THE
LAWS OF
THINKING

20 Secrets to Using the Divine Power of Your Mind to Manifest Prosperity

MASTER PROPHET

E. BERNARD JORDAN

HAY HOUSE, INC.
Carlsbad, California
London • Sydney • Johannesburg
Vancouver • Hong Kong • New Delhi

Published and distributed in the United States by: Hay House, Inc.: www.hayhouse.com • *Published and distributed in Australia by:* Hay House Australia Pty. Ltd.: www.hayhouse.com.au • *Published and distributed in the United Kingdom by:* Hay House UK, Ltd.: www.hayhouse.co.uk • *Published and distributed in the Republic of South Africa by:* Hay House SA (Pty), Ltd.: www.hayhouse.co.za • *Distributed in Canada by:* Raincoast: www.raincoast.com • *Published in India by:* Hay House Publishers India: www.hayhouse.co.in

Unless otherwise indicated, all Scripture quotations are from the New King James version of the Bible, © 1979, 1980, 1982, by Thomas Nelson, Inc., Nashville, Tennessee

The intent of the author is only to offer information of a general nature to help you in your quest for emotional and spiritual well-being. In the event you use any of the information in this book for yourself, which is your constitutional right, the author and the publisher assume no responsibility for your actions.

Originally published by Foghorn Publishers, 2006: **ISBN:** 0-9779452-2-7

Library of Congress Control Number: 2006937220

Hardcover ISBN: 978-1-4019-1796-8
Tradepaper ISBN: 978-1-4019-1799-9

11 10 09 08   8 7 6 5
1st Hay House edition, February 2007
5th edition, January 2008

Printed in the United States of America

DEDICATION

I would like to dedicate this book to my mentor in ministry Rev. Frederick Eikerenkoetter, *Th.B., D.Sc.L., Ph.D.* affectionately known as "Rev. Ike," to the members of P.O.M.E. which is the company of prophets trained in the fine and ancient arts of prophecy, and finally to my wife, Pastor Debra Jordan.

PROPHETIC PARTNERS

I would like to thank each of these prophetic partners. Their financial seeds have made this book a reality. Every time someone receives life through reading this work, may God add years and fruitfulness to your life.

Prophetess Lorna Aaron

Prophetess Ioana Beckford

Brother Calvin Brown

Carolyn Butts

Sister Debra Campany

Brother Edward Campany

Prophetess Mascareen Cohen

Brother Basil Gibbs

Bishop Yardley Griffin

Brother Dennis Green

Prophetess Alice P. Jackson

Pastor Debra Jordan

Prophetess Gloria Jean Kelley

Prophetess Willie Mae Parris

Sister Anndera Peeples

Pastor Tecoy Porter

Dr. Ellington Porter

Prophetess Lynetta Ruble

Michael Ruble

Father Joseph Simmons

Prophetess Justine Simmons

Dr. Cyclyn Smith-Mobley

Prophetess Marsha Mcghie-
   Steinberg

Bishop Shammah Womack

CONTENTS

———◆———

FOREWORD

*P*rosperity has gone from buzzword to cliché in the past decade. Pastors, parishioners, business owners, CEOs, athletes, and even entertainers all believe they know what prosperity is. When they attain their brand of prosperity, they begin to pursue their style of prosperous living without implementing a workable plan. For the most part, they arrive at the end of an exhausting journey and discover that they are no closer to their goal—and they really didn't know what their goal was in the first place.

In four centuries, the universal church has proscribed its followers from indulgences that were thought to corrupt moral character. In a sincere attempt to expurgate the bad, they have also thrown away the greatest good of all—our God-given ability to *think*. While many churches squirm like a fish out of water at the idea of independent thought, what they fail to realize is that the purpose of creation is directly connected to man's ability to think for himself. Salvation does not occur within the soul of humanity without the use of the mind. With the mouth confession is made, but with the mind, man believes.

Unfortunately, many religious leaders do not want their members to think. They fear that once they free their minds and begin asking difficult questions, they will discover that they are being manipulated and controlled. So some conservative Christian leaders scorn intellectualism and discourage thought, denying their flock the connection with their most godlike asset: their mind. Being a third-generation child of the Pentecostal heritage, I distinctly remember pastors strictly forbidding members to visit certain churches within our denomination, fearing that we might not come back.

Also, I remember how the same pastors encouraged us to read the Bible only, claiming that other books would contaminate our mind and spirit, rendering us worthless in the sight of God. Naturally that excluded books about science, technology, astronomy, medicine, or even law. For the most part, no one from our faith community ever entered the workforce in any of those disciplines. Most parishioners acquiesced and remained ignorant. Being an existentialist, I choose to read and reread works by some of the greatest thinkers in the world.

While many believed that I would come back from that experience contaminated and preaching false doctrine, just the opposite happened. I gained an appreciation for the Lord Jesus Christ as never before. For the first time in my life, I realized that Christ truly is all in all. I realized that God uses *minds*—as author Napoleon Hill would say, The Master Mind—to communicate truths beyond our limited understanding.

Should we accept what religious leaders tell us unquestioningly? Should we assume they have some special access to the truth that we cannot? The only way that we will know the answers to those questions is when we search for knowledge. Searching will require us to explore the many avenues that God has made available to us for our learning. Reading, questioning and acquiring knowledge is not counter to the desire of God; they are the *intent* of God.

> *Because they hated knowledge and did not choose the fear of the Lord. They would not accept my counsel, They spurned all my reproof.*
>
> — Proverbs 1:29-30 NASU

There is a direct correlation between reverencing God and loving knowledge. One cannot truly love God without also loving knowledge. The Creator is Knowledge, and He does not wish His creation to be ignorant. Despite your allegiance to church, family, and community, if you hate knowledge you will not know how to serve God. It is through knowledge that we understand the all sufficiency, all potency, and the omni-scientific mind of Elohim, Creator of heaven and earth.

> *The fear of the Lord is the beginning of knowledge; Fools despise wisdom and instruction.*
>
> — Proverbs 1:7 NASU

Over the years I have had the honor of meeting some of the worlds greatest spiritual and business leaders. The most inimitable is His Grace Bishop E. Bernard Jordan. Few, if any, of the leaders I have become acquainted with come close to his singularity of purpose. His life's mission is to empower his people. Who are his people? Jesus was once asked the same question; Bishop Jordan's response is the same: his people are those who do the will of the Father.

Bishop Jordan has written a stellar work that is guaranteed to free the mentally enslaved, acquit the wrongfully charged, and bring healing to the sick. *The Law of Thinking* is not a work for the shallow-minded person. It is demanding and challenging. It is neither intended to be used as the basis for unmerited criticism nor as sermon material for the minister having difficulty receiving a fresh word from the Lord. It was written with a very clear aim: to provoke spiritual thought. Bishop Jordan realizes that everything in life started with a thought. Bill Gates's Microsoft, Oprah Winfrey's Harpo Productions, Steven Spielberg's DreamWorks, Henry Ford's Ford Motor Company, and even his own Zoë Ministries all began with a thought.

Every invention, university, book, song, business, home, skyscraper, movie, stage play, and baby began when someone chose to think. Nothing happens without thought. Creation did not happen without God's Thought. Bishop Jordan's first objective is getting you to think. His second is to help you understand the laws that govern the universe of thought. And his final goal is to help you organize your thoughts into a system that will ensure positive results in your life. The winners in life are not necessarily Rhodes scholars or the most spiritual, but rather the people who solve the most problems for their fellow travelers.

Solving problems is the most lucrative profession in the universe, because everyone has problems. But to help others solve their problems effectively, you must have a workable, effective, easy to use, easy to teach system in place to solve your own problems. Without a system, you will fail. That is why so many entertainers and athletes go broke when just a few years before they were on top of the world. They had no system. This book contains that system: the Law of Thinking.

The Law is a set of principles that is organized and enforced by a governing authority. Break the law, and you will suffer unfortunate consequences. Obey the law, and you will experience freedom, prosperity and satisfaction. In *The Laws of Thinking: 20 Secrets to Using the Divine Power of Your Mind to Manifest Prosperity,* Bishop Jordan shows you how to tap into the freedom that you've always wanted to enjoy but never thought you could. You will reach your zenith when you discover the hidden truth: you don't have to search for God's mind. You already possess it. Keep reading and be transformed!

> *For who has known the mind of the Lord, that he will instruct him? But we have the mind of Christ.*
> — 1 Corinthians 2:16 NASU

Aaron D. Lewis, D.Min., Ph.D.
The Family of God, East Hartford, CT

"I'M SAVED, SO WHY AM I NOT PROSPEROUS?"

————◆————

L ife is learning, and one of the truths I am learning as I grow in prophecy and understanding of the reality of God's will and Spirit is that while faith is the heart of what it means to be human, it also has a downside. Faith, combined with ignorance, can breed a dangerous fatalism.

You almost certainly know someone like this: a person who is saved and is one of the children of the Lord, but who stands idly by and watches life and opportunity pass because they are "putting everything in God's hands." Such a person will often wonder—and I have had many people express this to me—why, even though they tithe and they attend church and they have accepted Christ as their Savior, why others get rich and live in mansions and drive fancy cars and they still struggle to pay their mortgage or still live in rented housing at age 40. They will ask me, "Why is God angry with me?"

I tell them the same thing: God is not angry with them, frustrated, perhaps. But then I share with them something many of them are not prepared to deal with: their prosperity or poverty lies not the hands of God, but in their hands. "The fault, dear Brutus, lies not within our stars, but within ourselves. . . ."[1] These people, who far and away are good, honest, compassionate people of faith, may love and serve God, but they do not *understand* God. They don't comprehend how God operates on this earthly plane. They fail to perceive that just as He created laws of physics, biology and chemistry for this world to operate within, He also created laws to govern Himself and the Spirit that resides within each of us. Yes, God is bound by laws of His own design; without them, all would be chaos.

What happens when you are ignorant of the laws of nature and you act without regard for them? You end up in trouble—jumping off a bridge because you think you can fly, or other such foolishness. And when you are ignorant of the Laws of God, you will also end up in trouble. You will wonder why good fortune, wealth and success come to others and not to you, even though you obey God with every breath. Well, here's the newsflash: God doesn't want you to obey Him. He wants you to obey yourself and fulfill the divine purpose He has already ordained for you. You can't do that if you're ignorant of how God works in this earthly realm.

The Laws of Thinking is a book about what I call "informed faith"—faith in God that is made all-powerful and fully realized by your awareness of the Laws that govern God's relationship with you and your relationship to the world. As you can gather from the title of the book, the Laws are all about what goes on in that fantastic structure between your ears: your mind. As you will

---

1. *Source:* http://www.amk.Ca/quotations/shakespeare/page 10

discover, your thoughts have the authority to shape the divine nature that resides within you, the "I Am" that makes you a co-creator with the Creator. Your divine power to create what you desire in this world lies dormant inside your mind, just as it lies dormant within every man and woman on this planet. When you fully perceive its presence and purpose—and more important, the patterns and habits of thinking that bring it forth—that power switches on. Life becomes a realm of infinite possibilities. Wealth, good people, opportunity, and the chance to change some aspect of the world . . . they all manifest. You *become* god.

As you can see, this knowledge can rock your world. It's mind-blowing and perception-expanding, and not everyone will be able to handle it. In fact, I'd say that the majority of Christians cannot handle the ideas in *The Laws of Thinking*. Why? Because it's frightening to suggest that God can be comprehended, that nothing is given to you just for showing up, and that to achieve your goals in this life you must discover your passion and purpose and work your ideas to make great things happen. That puts all the responsibility for success or failure squarely on your shoulders. Many folks can't handle that; they're too afraid. It's much easier for them to sit back and wait for God to throw blessings at them, like winning some sort of cosmic lottery. Fear paralyzes them, and as we'll see, fear is a useless emotion.

Which kind of Christian will you be? One of the fearful fatalists or one of the scholars of the Law, fully aware and ready to claim your birthright as God's junior partner, helping manifest your part of His vision for this world? What you desire most is already out there, waiting for you to bring it forth and claim it. In these pages, you're going to learn the secrets to doing exactly that.

The lessons in this book will enable you to:

- Realize your divine nature

- Understand God's purpose for you

- Gain control of unproductive thoughts and emotions

- Perceive people in your life who are damaging to your goals

- Understand the power and role of money

- Know how to attract the results you desire

- See portents of good things to come even in misfortune

- Peer into the secret machinery that governs the Universe

- Achieve the wealth and prosperity that awaits you

- And much more

Ready? Praise God, we're going to change your life forever and elevate you into informed faith. Amen.

One final note: if you want to deepen your studies into these matters, pick up a copy of an incredible book we have used as a study guide, *The Miracle of Right Thought,* by Orison Swett Marden. You can find it at **www.zoeministries.com**.

— E. Bernard Jordan

Chapter 1

THE LAW OF BECOMING

—◦—

Then the Lord said to Moses, "See, I have made you like God to Pharaoh, and your brother Aaron will be your prophet."

— Exodus 7:1

Who are you? You may have thought you knew the answer to that question, but you probably did not. Don't tell me your name; that's what you're called, not who you are. Until you know who you are, you will not understand where you belong. Once you know who you are, it will become abundantly clear *why* you are here on earth, in your body, at this time.

Let's begin this exploration by looking at one of the most famous scenes from the Old Testament: Moses speaking to the burning bush. In this passage of the Bible, Moses hears the voice of God speaking to him from a bush that burns but is not consumed. Aware that the bush's not being consumed is a miracle,

1

Moses humbles himself before the Lord and receives the charge that will change his life: liberating the Hebrews from bondage.

In Exodus 3:13-14, Scripture says, *Moses said to God, "Suppose I go to the Israelites and say to them, 'The God of your fathers has sent me to you,' and they ask me, 'What is his name?' Then what shall I tell them?" God said to Moses, "I am who I am. This is what you are to say to the Israelites: 'I AM has sent me to you.'"* In those two words, "I Am," reside the wholeness of your true nature. God placed you in this world not to wait around for Him to put things into your hands, but for you to declare "I Am" yourself! When you state "I Am," you declare not just who you are, but what your purpose is. They are one and the same. This is one of the essential truths of the Laws of Thinking:

∼

WHEN YOU DECLARE "I AM," YOU BECOME GOD.

∼

Your Divine Nature

Ignorant minds will look at that statement and call it blasphemy, but that is only because they do not truly understand the nature of the relationship between God and man. Each and every one of us was created in God's image; there is nothing in God that does not exist in man, and nothing in man that does not exist in God. You were sent here by "I Am", and "I Am" is the state of your mind and your imagination. There is divinity in you, if you can see it.

Wow. That is a huge idea, maybe the hugest of ideas. You are god. But when you think about it, is it really so far-fetched? Man is the only creature with the power to create and shape his world, to bring things into being by first thinking them into being (because all things begin in the mind) and then working to manifest them into physical reality. Who else has the power to create what did not exist before? God, of course! When you declare your "I Am" nature, you are claiming your divine birthright and stepping into your role as God's proxy in this world. You begin to discover your purpose, which is to walk in divinity and declare God's will to men through your works and your actions.

What does this mean? It means that in the same way that God's declaration becomes reality, your declaration becomes reality. When you state "I Am," you inherit the same power to make your thoughts manifest in this reality. In this way, you move beyond want, which is the source of misery and poverty of the spirit, as Buddha knew. Instead of wanting and coveting, walk in your divine nature:

~

IF YOU DESIRE THE THING, DECLARE YOURSELF TO BE THE THING AND IT WILL MANIFEST.

~

If you desire a fine house, you must be the house. If you desire to be the owner of a prosperous company, you must declare yourself to be that company. There is no difference between your being and that company, house or whatever else is your passionate desire. That is your divine power, granted to you as part of your being by the Father! There is no greater inheritance.

People Will Scorn You for Not Being Consumed

Now Moses was tending the flock of Jethro his father-in-law, the priest of Midian, and he led the flock to the far side

*of the desert and came to Horeb, the mountain of God.
There the angel of the LORD appeared to him in flames of
fire from within a bush. Moses saw that though the bush
was on fire it did not burn up.*

— Exodus 3:1-2

When you claim your "I Am" nature, you will be as God in that burning bush: on fire, but not consumed. This will be wondrous to you, as you feel your awareness of prophecy and God's purpose in your life open up like a flower within you, and as you walk daily in the Word knowing you are progressing toward the destiny God ordained for you even when the Universe was formed. But when other people perceive your divine nature, they will be confused. They will see that you are as the burning bush, but that you are not consumed.

> *When you claim your "I Am" nature, you will be as God in that burning bush: on fire, but not consumed.*
>
>

You see, most people can't see God in man. They crave miracles, but they want to see miracles that involve seas parting or plagues of locusts (preferably raining down on people they don't like), and they fail to realize that the true miracle is the opening of the eyes of a person like yourself. The miracle is that you are god, and that you can be in flesh, declaring yourself to be god and yet not be consumed by the Spirit within you. How is that possible? That's the miracle. When your "I Am" consciousness becomes aware of itself, you can live and walk in Spirit and yet not be consumed by it. By becoming aware of the Spirit within you, you *become* that Spirit. That consciousness is a flame-retardant suit that lets you influence the Spirit to create the works of God without being burned by it.

Do not be put aside from your purpose or discouraged by people who do not or cannot understand the nature of your true self, even as they cannot look away from the fire. The path of each life is a choice, and some will choose to become aware after you do, and others will never be aware at all. Do not pity them, but also do not listen to their negative or doubting words. Be true to your divine truth.

Are You Aware of God's Nature?

The teachings in this part of the book are the foundation for all that comes later. The simple, cosmic truth is that God wants you to walk in divinity and experience Him the way you're supposed to: as His partner in bringing the Word into flesh in this world. This goes against many traditions that insist God is angry, punitive and always seeking a reason to cast man into Hell. That's absurd. If you are a reflection of everything that exists in God, why would He cast rage and retribution at Himself? Why would He damn himself? Learning the Laws of Thinking turns many traditional Christian teachings on their heads and reveals them for what they really are: methods of controlling fearful, small-minded people.

When you wake up and start partaking of God's true nature, you begin partaking of your own true nature. Or to say it another way:

IF YOU'RE NOT AWARE OF GOD'S NATURE, YOU'RE NOT AWARE OF YOUR OWN NATURE.

You won't know who and what you are (and who and what you can *become*) until you understand who and what God is. You can only partake of a revelation that you have received. As long as you are walking in a state of unawareness, you cannot have the things that God has decreed for you.

God is Not a Noun

Whoa. I just blew your mind, didn't I? Get used to it—that's going to happen a lot in *The Laws of Thinking*. But it's true: God is not a noun. A noun is a person, place or thing, and God is all of the above, but above all, God is a Force, a Mind, an Intellect, and a Spirit. That Spirit exists for one reason above all others: *to manifest change in the world.* So if you take that idea to its logical conclusion, you come to this:

∽

GOD IS A VERB.

∽

God is an action word. Remember, God states that His name is "I Am." "I Am" is an action phrase that stems from the verb "to be." So to be god—which is what you are—is to be. When you come into your "I Am" awareness, you are in action as god. God is action. God in you is a force to take action to create change in this physical reality. God is the action itself. Once you are in an "I Am" state of being, you are the action *yourself.*

What does that mean? It means that once you declare your "I Am," you claim both the power and the responsibility to act on manifesting God's will on earth. When you say "I Am," you have just taken on a new acting role, with God waiting to see the new action you are about to take. You are the actor, writer, director, producer, and the cause of all things.

You must produce your cause, but make sure it's in line with God's cause. If it's a contrary cause, you will get contrary results. John 10:30 says, *"I and the Father are one."* You must be in alignment of purpose with God if your actions are to bring forth the manifestations He desires. That's critically important. That's why it is vital to suppress your intellect and your ego even as you are proclaiming yourself to be "I Am." Even as you partake of the divinity that God has granted you, you must not try to impose your own will on what God desires of you. You must be open to hearing God and to producing and creating what He has in mind for you to create.

You must be in alignment of purpose with God if your actions are to bring forth the manifestations He desires.

~

When you can set aside ego (not an easy thing for anyone to do) and keep your mind still and at peace, you open yourself to being a conduit of ideas that come to you directly from God. As long as there is that agreement of mind and purpose, you experience the constant, eternal inflow of ideas and inspiration from God.

You end up copying from the Source. It's like having the smartest kid in class always sitting next to you, always letting you copy off his homework! You wake in the morning alive with anointing and a flood of new ideas, new things to build and create, new opportunities to sow and give, new wealth coming your way. It's a thrilling way to live and to serve the intent of the Lord.

We Live in a Universe of Becoming

A little way back, I gave you an incomplete definition. I told you that "I Am" was taken from the verb "to be," but that's only partially true. "I Am" is also derived from the verb "to become." I held this back because it was a little too soon to share it with you, but you're ready for the revelation now. This is the revelation, the first of the Laws of Thinking:

~

LAW #1: WE LIVE NOT IN A UNIVERSE OF BEING, BUT OF BECOMING.

~

Nothing that lives is static. God is not static. He did not just create the world eons ago and then sit back and never change. God is EVOLVING; He is changing His being, His ideas, and His purposes all the time. God is *becoming*. And because you were created in God's image with all things in you that are god, you are also becoming. If you stand still, if you are only being, then you are dead. We don't live in a Universe that was made; we live in a Universe that is *being* made, every moment.

Everything comes in stages. Everything and everyone is evolving, changing, and becoming something new, moving toward what it will be tomorrow. And when it reaches that state, guess what? It begins to become what it will be the next day! Every moment, you are moving toward a new state of being—either toward fulfillment of your potential as determined by God or away from that fulfillment. The choice is yours, but you can never stop moving. You are always on the road to becoming someone other than who you are at this very moment. The question you must ask is:

~

"WHO AM I BECOMING?"

~

There's blessed freedom and joy in the fact of becoming. You are never trapped in where or what you are. You are never stuck in a state of poverty, ill health or loneliness . . . unless you choose to be. That is the message of "I Am." When you declare yourself to be god, you are taking responsibility for your becoming. Isn't God in charge? Then why should anyone else be in charge of saving you from a life that is not what you hoped it would be? The harsh reality is, no one will save you. That's not the job of the prophets, your friends, your family, anyone. It's not God's job. His task is to lay the path before you and say, "Here, I have ordained this for you to follow." Whether or not you follow is entirely up to you.

Becoming empowers us to change what we are and our lot in life. If it didn't, people who started off poor would not become billionaire owners of huge corporations or world-famous rap superstars. They would remain on their dirt farms, or end up dead or in prison. Instead, they understood that their destiny was to become, that becoming empowered them to change their reality.

Go Back to the Word

To become, you must discover your "I Am," and to do that you must go back to the Word. You must be at peace, rest your thoughts and your ego, and listen to the voice of God speaking to you. If you do not do this, then you will condemn yourself to live in a Universe of the past, like a still photo of the way your life once was. You will be stuck. The Universe as it is in God's mind is a motion picture, one that He is always editing—and that you, as God's partner, are helping him edit. If God is the Master Editor, you in your "I Am" state of mind are His apprentice.

For some people, the concept of becoming and of an evolving, changing God is difficult to accept. It makes them feel more secure to think that God stopped with the Bible, which He never changed. But if we mirror God, then look how much the world of men has changed in the thousands of years since the stories in the Bible took place. Does it not make sense that God would change as well?

. . . we are in a constant state of creation.

And anyway, we are in a constant state of creation. Our bodies create new cells every moment. We replace all the trillions of cells in our bodies every seven years. We are constantly being reborn in flesh, and because of God's love, we are constantly reborn in spirit. That love gives every cell a second chance, a third chance, a fourth chance to awaken to the truth of "I Am" and realize its true potential. Every morning, you are renewed and healed. You have a brand new day to change the world.

Are You a "Favor-ite?"

In the Bible, you can read about the many tribes that lived in the land where Moses led the Hebrews after their escape from slavery: the Hittites, Jebusites, Canaanites and so on. But what if there was a new tribe, and what if membership was based not on your bloodline, but on your ability to be at one with the Word and the purpose of God, to allow God to manifest through you? What if declaring and living your "I Am" status gained you entry into this elite group? You would become a "Favor-ite," one upon whom God has cast His grace and favor.

When you become a Favor-ite, a season of grace and favor will be upon you. Good things will come into your life without you having seemed to work for them; you were busy sowing or giving money or working to develop an idea in another area, and money just showed up at your door. And people will say, "How did you do that?" More important, they will say, "Why does he get that when I'm working so hard and I get nothing?" Just smile inside yourself and know a fundamental truth of God's order of things:

~

FAVOR ISN'T FAIR.

~

That's right. Favor doesn't come to those who earn it through the sweat of their brow, and it doesn't come to those who do nothing more than sit in church, never give more than the minimum and sit back and wait for God to smile upon them. God looks with pity on them, because they don't get it. Favor only comes to those who *understand how God operates in this world*. Favor is not fair. Some people will hate you because of this inequity, but you have to be able to withstand their censure and still declare "I Am" even if they say you are arrogant. Because whose favor matters more: God's or your neighbor's?

How God Operates

I've saved the most important idea for the end of this chapter, because it's going to shape the rest of the material to come. I've said that the key to favor and to realizing the potential that God has preordained for your life lies in understanding how God operates in this world—comprehending the Laws He has created and therefore must follow. That fact can be boiled down to this statement:

~

THE PURPOSE OF HUMAN EXISTENCE IS TO EXPRESS THE PURPOSE OF THE SPIRIT OF GOD IN THE MATERIAL WORLD.

~

Wow! That's a huge idea! That would mean that instead of being put here by God to scurry around like ants, as some Christians would have you believe, God puts each of us here to play a role in bringing forth the physical manifestation of God's plan. Each person plays a part in bringing to fruition a part of that blueprint. God is the Prime Architect, and each of us is the architect of our own existences, thinking things into being with the power of our minds. That is why God created Man: to play his role in bringing forth the myriad parts of God's eternal purpose. To put it another way:

~

THE WHOLE AIM OF CREATION IS MANIFESTATION.

~

If that's not earth-shaking enough for you, try this: God needs you. He needs us all. You see, God is not flesh. He is Spirit. The purpose of Spirit is to express, but because Spirit is not flesh, it cannot express itself on this material plane. It needs a vessel to fill, and then the Spirit can guide that vessel to express its purpose. Notice that the word "manifestation" even begins with the word "man."

That is why God created us and the cosmos: to express His purpose in material reality! That's a thrilling, humbling responsibility, isn't it? The purpose of human existence is to express the purpose of Spirit—to make it manifest in the material realm. But to do that, you must understand that you are also spirit. You are a walking, talking spirit clothed in a suit of flesh and blood, and it is that spirit that makes you one with God.

Many people cannot feel or hear their spirit speaking within them, and so they do not speak with the voice of Spirit. That is why it is so important to be at peace and still—to quiet your mind and the chaos of your thoughts, intellect, worry and fear—so that you can hear the Spirit speaking within you. When you become fully aware of that Spirit—when you pay it full attention—you call it forth and can then claim your "I Am" state of being. You become *spirit ex primo*, spirit pressed out. Man is simply God pressed out into this world through flesh. When you hear and embrace the Spirit that you share with God, your words press His thoughts out, and you express the light of God within you.

That is why it is so crucial to always be thinking about wealth, prosperity, health, peace and so on. When you are speaking in Spirit, your words will manifest, for good or ill. You are here on this earth to manifest your "I Am" and to go forth and bring God's vision to life. Your aim is to *become* god.

How's that for a first chapter? There's a lot more to come.

* * *

SUMMARY

- You have a divine nature that you share with God.

- You must realize "I Am" in order to manifest. You must become the things you want.

- God is an action.

- We live in a Universe of becoming. You are always becoming something.

- Favor isn't fair.

- You were created by God to manifest his vision.

- You are spirit.

- Your purpose is to become god.

Chapter 2

THE LAW OF SPIRIT

———◦◦———

The Spirit himself testifies with our spirit that we are God's children.

— Romans 8:16

Let's talk about fear. Fear is a useless emotion. Think of the word FEAR as standing for False Evidence Appearing Real. That means when you feel fear about doing something, it's because something is lying to your eyes and ears and making you believe you do not have what it takes to reach a goal or bring success into your life. Fear is a self-fulfilling prophecy, the closest thing to the devil reaching into your life to wreak havoc and cause you misery. Of course, as with all things involving the Laws of Thinking, you have to *choose* to let fear become a factor in your life. If you do, then you reap the results, just as you do when you approach your life with confidence and trust in God.

Fear brings pain and struggle to your life because it prevents you from taking actions that benefit you and fulfill the vision of the Almighty, but that's not fear's greatest effect. The most damaging effect of fear comes in the mind. Here's something you should know:

~

THE MIND ACTS ON THE IMPULSE OF THE STRONGEST SUGGESTION GIVEN TO IT.

~

Whatever you are focusing on, that is what will come into being. You must be focused on what comes from your spirit in order to control the suggestion that influences your mind, or you will be subject to negative suggestions from your mind and the world. What have you been suggesting to your mind? Fear and worry? Or confidence and faith? Whatever thoughts dominate your mind, that is what you will bring into existence in the world of thoughts, and what becomes thought eventually becomes material. If you are living in poverty or material want, it's probably because you're living in the physical manifestation of your fears!

Where Are You Blocking Spirit?

When you open your mind to the Word and the purpose of God, you work in Spirit, and creating the prosperity and opportunity you desire in your life becomes much easier. You see, Spirit is the original creative force; Spirit exists to manifest on this physical plane. So when you are operating fearlessly and boldly in Spirit, you do not need to work to create the result you want. Spirit will create them for you. Money and financial opportunity will flow into your hands seemingly without effort, because when you remove all the barriers from Spirit and let it work through you, it is like a river of good fortune rushing right at you.

But what about when you struggle? When you think you are operating in Spirit and you know you have listened to God's Word and are working in unison with Him? What's going on then? Well, it probably means that you have let worry creep into your thinking. When you struggle to manifest your desires, or when you just hit rough patches in life, it is because you are fighting the purpose of Spirit in you. Your ego is getting in the way of God's purpose. It's as if you're saying, "Wait, Lord, I know how to do this better."

Worry, stress, doubt—these are all ways of essentially saying you don't trust God.

Let me tell you this: it's folly to ask God how He's going to manifest blessings and favor in your life, and even more foolish to try to tell God how it should happen. God wants to work with you as a conduit for Him to manifest on earth; He doesn't want you to tell Him how to be God. Worry, stress, doubt—these are all ways of essentially saying you don't trust God. God wants to be trusted. When you worry or doubt, you block the working of Spirit. Worry constipates the manifestation of Spirit. Everything has a flow, but stress, fear, anxiety . . . they block that flow. In a way:

WORRY IS MEDITATION IN THE WRONG DIRECTION: NEGA-TATION.

Struggle is the Universe's way of teaching you to let go of your ego and quit blocking the Spirit that is working through you. When you struggle, you're reminded to quit fighting, trust God, let go of the wheel and let Him drive. Are things in your life not manifesting? Where could you be blocking Spirit?

The Power of Naming

We'll take a closer look at this later in the book, but it's important to mention it here. Part of the Law of Spirit is the power of naming. The secret and the power to living are knowing the name of who you are and what you want. This is an ancient idea that predates Christianity: once you know the true name of something, you can express its nature and command it. The name of a thing is the first, most basic expression of its spirit. When you want to work in Spirit, first you must know and say the name of who or what you are trying to manifest in this world.

This goes back to the concept of declaring your "I Am"-ness and partaking of your divine nature. But it goes even further. You must also name the things you want in your mind. That freezes them there and allows Spirit to go to work manifesting them in physical reality. That manifestation can take time, but if you are patient, the manifestation will come. Remember, don't ask God how long it will take. Just trust that it will come.

Do you know the names of the things you want to manifest in your life? If not, you need to start thinking about that today. Right now.

Embracing Your Sonship

We all know that Jesus was the Son of God. But He's also called the Son of Man. Why is that? Because you are god, and so Jesus is as much the offspring of Man as of the Creator. This introduces the concept of "sonship." We are called children of God, but what does that mean?

In our walk as believers, we grow in three stages of sonship:

1. Infancy, in which we can make no choices and are basically slaves of the actions of others.

2. Children of God, where we can begin to understand more about God and Spirit but still have no power to choose.

3. Mature sons (and daughters) of God. Here we have the ability, should we use it, to see the things the Father wants us to begin to know.

In time, we can come into what God is calling us into—our potential as leaders, artists, entrepreneurs, writers, parents, and beyond. When we fully understand what God wants of us and how we are to manifest it, we become something else: *Heirs of God*. All people are children of God; only a select few ever become His Heirs. They have passed through trials to learn and grow into the fullness of their status as co-equals with Jesus as sons of God.

There I go again, blowing your mind! Well, what if I told you that the Universe is waiting for you to manifest as god? When you become a true son of God, all the Universe and the creatures within it are waiting to yield to you! You only need to come to a place where that yielding can happen. Here's something most people never even comprehend:

~

YOU ARE ALREADY AT ONE WITH GOD.

~

Separation from God does not exist. Everything is within the Infinite Mind. The only separation from God exists in your mind. That is the only sin in the world. As you progress toward sonship, you will begin to perceive that you are inside, not outside.

You Are the Captain of Your Soul

Has your world been rocked in just a chapter and a half? Good, because what I'm trying to do is lay to rest some of the more poisonous ideas circulating in the church these days. One of my goals is to help you understand that you are the captain of your soul:

It matters not how strait the gate, how charged with punishments the scroll, I am the master of my fate; I am the captain of my soul.

> *"Invictus,"*
> *by William Earnest Henley*

God sets the path before you and creates the Laws by which you can succeed; He leaves it to you to select which path you will walk. To do otherwise would make you a puppet. Choice is power, and you must risk making the wrong choice to come into your power. Making choices and dealing with the consequences is the way you realize who you are as a being. Until there is realization, there is no manifestation.

The Law of Spirit

At the core of everything we're talking about is Spirit. Spirit is the captain of your soul, not personality. Personality is what resides in your intellect, and your intellect can make you question the will of God. When you act from intellect, you are seeing your-self as separate from God. When you act in Spirit, you are one with God.

The Law of Spirit is this:

~

LAW #2: SPIRIT SEEKS TO MANIFEST IN OUR REALITY, BUT IT CAN ONLY DO SO THROUGH MAN.

~

The purpose of Spirit is always to self-express, but Spirit—including God—has no physical self, so it cannot manifest on its own. God is pure Spirit; that is why the Creation occurred. Spirit is always seeking self-expression through manifestation. Spirit has goals; it is not static. But the only way Spirit can have mani-festation is through us! Spirit moves forward and has a future, but to manifest it must do so in evolving beings—you and me.

That means man's purpose is to be the vessel for Spirit. That's a thrilling reality and an enormous charge, something you should take very seriously. The fact is, only man can move creation for-ward. Only man, working in Spirit, knows what to do with creation. That is where the difference between being and becoming comes into play. When Spirit has no physical being through which to express itself, it is stuck being. But when it passes into a willing ves-sel—a man or woman obedient to the will of God and attuned to the voice of God—Spirit passes out of being and into becoming. Once we understand that we and our Father are one, we also pass from being into becoming. Spirit *becomes* through us.

The reverse is also true. All things aspire to become, but to do so, they must become Spirit. Until you become Spirit and declare your "I Am" to all, you are only being. You are static, unmoving in the fabric of God's plan. But when you become Spirit, you start to become. You evolve, move forward, create, and begin to draw to you those good things that God has already placed in your future: money, success, recognition.

You Are a Speaking Spirit

The truth becomes even more astonishing when you consider this: when you bring your mind to a place of peace and quiet, God talks to you. Well, Spirit can only speak to spirit. So you must already be a spirit! In fact, that is exactly what you are:

~

YOU ARE A SPEAKING SPIRIT PASSING FROM BEING TO BECOMING.

~

Amen! You are a speaking spirit speaking back to God. God created you in his image and likeness; if God is Spirit, so is Man. Your body is simply a vessel for your spirit to pass from being to becoming. It's a tool for the spirit, allowing your mind, personality and body to shape the spirit and lead it to that state of becoming. You are a luminous being whose existence transcends this temporary cloak of flesh that you wear.

That Spirit is already present in you, a creative, titanic source of power to effect change, waiting for you to discover it. It has been since you were born. At the date and time of your birth, your spirit incarnated itself in you, longitude and latitude coming together at a time in the heavens and a place on earth. At that moment, the spirit inhabiting you moved from being to becoming. That is where the Spirit's, and your, journey begins. You are always in motion relative to your manifestation as Spirit, either toward it or away from it.

Everything is Spirit

Ancient alchemists told that the world was created of four essential elements—air, earth, fire and water—with an invisible element, the ether, present to bind everything together. They were more right than they knew: Spirit is the unseen element that underlies everything on this physical plane. Just as when you touch a solid object you are not touching solid matter but the electrical charges in the empty space between electrons, when you experience anything in this world, you are experiencing Spirit.

> *Spirit is the unseen element that underlies everything on this physical plane.*
> ⮿

How is this possible? Think about the fact that nothing exists until first created in the mind of God or Man. The Spirit is that creative mind, acting to create without reservation the image that it has presented to itself. Your mind is always acting to create. It is always bringing forth a creative act. Your mind is creation in manifestation.

Being or thought manifests objectively from an invisible Universe, brought forth from the invisible, from thought to form. You are always moving from thought to form. The Word is creation, and Spirit is always moving to find a form, a vessel to manifest itself in. That vessel is you, manifesting the Word, God's power of creation. The Word existed before Time, and thought brought Time into being. In the same way, you are moving from Word to form through Spirit. You must think like a millionaire—speak the Word of wealth—before you can form a million dollars. Everything starts with the Word and ends up in form. You were once the thought of your parents, and you ended up in form. To put this complex idea more simply:

~

GOD = WORD = SPIRIT = THOUGHT = CREATION = MANIFESTATION

~

When I say everything is Spirit, I mean everything. Everything you eat, touch, see, hear or wear is Spirit. Spirit is the idea and the energy of creation that formed everything in this world and will form everything to come. If something doesn't exist yet in form, it does exist in Spirit if you have thought it! That is the incredible power of thought. There are infinite ways to express that Spirit, but only one mind at the source: God, the Infinite Mind.

Money, too, is pure Spirit. In fact, money is the purest form of Spirit at work. Money is, after all, the power of change, and that is why Spirit manifests: to express itself through change. Tell me what change is possible without money? You'll be thinking a long time. When we see change in the world, we are seeing the effect of money. Money brings thought into form; it is the tool through which Spirit manifests in the corporeal realm.

The highest form of money is "I Am." When you state "I Am money," you bring money to you. You must have the boldness to come before the throne and declare that all is Spirit and pull from that realm. When you can do that, doors will open. You will be able to give without thinking about reward, and you will create without worrying about money. You will operate purely in Spirit, inspired by the voice of God within you. You will manifest that which you desire most.

That is why people who truly operate in Spirit are not covetous people. When you acknowledge that all is Spirit, you have no business coveting. When you covet, you're saying you're too lazy to manifest something. You'd rather steal it. But when Spirit guides you, you can say to anyone, "Anything I need, you don't have," because only Spirit can meet your needs. You manifest the things you need. That's what I call getting to the root of prosperity, and like I like to say:

~

WHEN YOU GET TO THE ROOT, YOU'LL GET THE FRUIT.

~

The Benefits of Operating in Spirit

In the end, God's favor will only come to those who embrace Spirit and take action according to the Word that Spirit brings to them. Situations and challenges might make you forget for a time that you are Spirit. Life will intrude and you may feel yourself filled with doubt and worry. That is normal, but it is important in that case for you to remember who and what you are and declare who and what you are. Remember that you are "I Am." Once you recall that you are Spirit, you will change this world.

There are many other benefits to acting in Spirit:

- You gain the power to imagine, build and manifest. No other creature in the Universe possesses that Godlike power. Want to invent a new kind of automobile engine? Imagine it and do it! Want to write music that will move nations and produce wealth for you and your family? Imagine it and do it! Ideas are currency and ideas create wealth. Ideas come from God.

- God talks to you. Spirit can only talk to Spirit, so God needs somebody to talk to. When He talks to you, He's really talking to Himself!

- You will not become angry or discouraged. Spirit does not feel those stress-creating emotions that derail you from your purpose. Spirit just IS. When you are operating in Spirit, you will not become fearful that you are moving in the wrong direction or that the things you desire will not come to you. When Spirit directs you, it is impossible NOT to attain the objects of your desire.

- You will become a shape-shifter. When Jesus made the people of the synagogue angry, they took him to the brow of a hill and were going to cast him off the cliff to his death, but instead he passed among them and went his way. How did he do that? Because he was Spirit and was able to pass through circumstances and be untouched by them. You will become able to do that. There will always be someone seeking to throw you off course, but when you understand that you are Spirit, you will be able to go your own way and no one will be able to stop you.

Perhaps most wonderful of all, you will be one with God. You become god. You become one with the Source of all.

Do Not Worry About People's Anger

A final word: when you tell people that you are Spirit, many will become angry. More to the point, when you begin to manifest

26

the things and successes in your life that they covet, they will resent you. Small, petty people always resent the good fortune of others. Also, those who are saved but do not understand the Laws of Thinking and the methods of God will resent you as you ascend to the higher levels of thinking. When you challenge people's ignorance, you will raise their ire.

> *You see, everything you have the potential to manifest in this world has been laid down since the Creation.*
>
> ∽

It should not surprise you when I tell you that when you are obeying the Law of Spirit, the wrath of others does not matter. Men will always lead you to the brow of the hill; you must always pass and go your own way. Don't get caught up in their fear and anger. You will always be tested to see whether you're seeing it their way or God's way. Struggle is a reminder that God's way is the only way to achieve your potential.

They Were Talking About You

These are huge ideas with cosmic implications. But these Laws have been in motion since before the Creation. In fact, there was something said about you at the Creation, perhaps even before. You see, everything you have the potential to manifest in this world has been laid down since the Creation. You have the freedom to determine the form and amount of what you manifest when you are working in the Spirit, but God put it there for you before Time itself existed. That's why we need prophets—so we can understand what was being said about us in the beginning.

The reality of God and Spirit transcends what we think we know about Time, destiny and the Universe.

Once you understand the Alpha, you can understand how to move to the Omega. Once you understand the journey, you *become* the journey. That is an exhilarating, rewarding transcendent way to live and to do God's work.

* * *

SUMMARY

- Fear is a useless emotion.
- The mind acts on the impulse of the strongest suggestion given to it.
- You are at one with God.
- You are the captain of your soul.
- You are a speaking spirit.
- Spirit can only manifest through Man.
- Money is Spirit.
- When you get to the root, you'll get the fruit.
- When you operate in Spirit, you will become a shape-shifter.

Chapter 3

THE LAW OF
ATTRACTION

———•———

Resentment kills a fool, and envy slays the simple.

— Job 5:2

The Laws of Thinking are being revealed to you in this book and my teachings for one reason: to empower you to manifest the prosperity in your life that God has spoken for you. When you embrace this wisdom, good things are going to come into your life. And the harsh reality is that when that happens, people are going to be envious of you. They will be envious of your favor (never mind that favor isn't fair) and of your money and of your sense of clear purpose. They will wish they had what you had, and they will wish they expressed Spirit through themselves as you express Spirit through yourself.

Understand this: envy is not evil. God did not create anything evil. Envy is a sign that God is expressed through you. The true sin is want, covetousness, the desire by others to possess what you have manifested and the knowledge that they cannot because they have not allowed themselves to listen to God and become "I Am." Take their envy as a compliment, because it means they see what you yourself may not even be able to see: God within you.

"God Thinks He Is Me!"

You have a purpose here on earth. When people ask if there is a meaning to life, you can answer, "Yes, and I know what it is." Heads will turn and people will lean in to hear what you have to say. When they do, tell them, "The meaning of life is to manifest the good work of God in the physical realm." Tell them that your purpose is to manifest the truth that "I Am god." Some of them won't understand, but that's their problem. You don't have time to explain; you have manifesting to do!

I learned much about my faith and the words of the Lord at the feet of the great Reverend Ike, who was and is as charismatic a man as ever stepped to the front of a church. Rev. Ike understood the paradox of man being god. Once, a parishioner, taken aback by what he saw as Rev. Ike's ego, said, "Reverend Ike thinks he's God!" And Rev. Ike turned and shouted, "No! God thinks He is me!" That's a perfect comeback, but also a perfect message. The idea that there is any separation between you and God is patently false. You are God's expression. He cannot exist on this plane without you. That is why you were created. As the son is the expression of the father, you are the expression of God. You are the same.

When the Word Absolutely, Positively Has to Be There Overnight

You are God's missionary in this world. If you run into someone claiming to be God's messenger or missionary, surprise him and say, "Really? Me too!" Because that is what you are: God's

Federal Express service on the corporeal plane. You are the package that carries His will and expresses it in the world. And the beauty is, you don't have to do it overnight! You can take a lifetime—you operate on God's timetable.

The package you're carrying? God's Word. God's Word in the form of your word. Remember, when you claim your "I Am" birthright, you become co-equal to God, and your Word gains the power of His Spirit. Your word determines your day, who you are, where you are, and where you are bound. The Word is power to shape reality, so you should never think or say what you do not want to come into being. Exercise the power of the Word with the utmost care. It is a loaded gun and a slot machine about to pay off, both at the same time.

> *Your word determines your day, who you are, where you are, and where you are bound.*
>
>

When you name something, you give it a nature. When you say something, it takes on that form. Its reality reflects your perspective. The Word becomes flesh for you. When God created the Universe, He created it first in His Mind; it was only later, when He spoke, that it became flesh.

Buying What You Desire By Paying Attention

We come to this chapter having learned about the power of Spirit to make us embrace our oneness with God and our becoming a being with the ability to create as God. Now, it's time to talk about the forces that attract what you think about into your physical reality.

THE LAWS OF THINKING

As I said before, God is bound by the Laws that He created to govern both the realm of Spirit and our material realm. One of those Laws is that you cannot get something for nothing; you must always pay for what you receive. By this logic, if you want to manifest the money, opportunity and happiness you desire in life, you must give something for it. You must make a deposit in the bank of the Universe. If you go to a bank and try to make a withdrawal without having made a deposit, you'd better be wearing a ski mask; that's called robbery, and you'll go to prison for it. You must pay to play, and the only currency that's accepted in the Universe is of the world of Spirit. The money of this world is no good.

What must you pay in order to begin manifesting good things in your life? You must pay a price called *attention*. That's where the expression "pay attention" comes from! Here's a crucial truth to learn and remember:

~

THE KEY TO MANIFESTATION IS FOCUSING YOUR ATTENTION POWERFULLY AND PERSISTENTLY ON WHAT YOU DESIRE.

~

Each time you focus your attention on something, sending your energy and concentration out into the Spirit realm, you begin to draw it closer to you. You begin to make your thoughts manifest. You enhance your perception and increase your ability to be, do and have. Focused attention that does not faint or waver is sending a constant stream of creative energy into the future, declaring "I Am" to what you desire to bring into being. Attention is magnetism that attracts whatever it falls on to itself!

You can see, once again, how important it is that if you are to be a successful person—a "Favor-ite"—you must learn to govern your mind and banish thoughts of fear, doubt and negativity. Imagine if in a weak moment you allowed your attention to focus on something that would bring ruin onto yourself or your business—the idea of theft, the fear of illness, the risk of a bold enterprise that you are otherwise sure about. Who knows what result you might attract to you? It might be nothing; then again, it might be disastrous. In this way, we see that becoming "I Am" means putting your mind through some serious training!

Persistence is All

To those who by persistence in doing good seek glory, honor and immortality, he will give eternal life.
— Romans 2:7

We can't leave our discussion of attention without talking about persistence and its opposite, distraction. To employ the power of attention to manifest good, you must apply it with persistence. You must remain focused over time in order to allow Spirit to create and bring forth what you have envisioned in your mind and set in motion with your words. If you speak a word and then move your mind and your attention to something else, your vision will not have the chance to form from the incorporeal. Persistence of thought, word and focus is all-important to getting what you want . . . and doing what God wants of you!

Vision will not disappoint or deceive you. It will always tell you the truth and leave it to you what to do. You won't receive any signs in the heavens telling you to hold fast and stick to your course; you must trust in God to do that. What test of faith would it be if when you found the right course to prosperity, even if it didn't appear to be promising, if angels descended and said, "Yes, you're right!" Any fool could be a prophet if things were that transparent. God asks you to trust in Him and your own vision.

Like a woman expecting a child, every vision has to have a period of expectancy. It grows, forms and prepares. It will not deceive you. That's why it's called *conception*, not *deception*. The gestation period of any idea or vision is critical. If you interrupt it, you will abort it. You will interrupt the manifestation, and things will fall apart. You must allow gestation to continue and to allow the appointed time to come.

Distraction is the Enemy

In this context, distraction could also be termed *destruction*, because what distracts you from a single-minded focus on your goals will destroy the progress Spirit has been making in pulling those goals into material existence. A stray word, thought or loss of attention can ruin what may have been years in the making. That is why after the angel Gabriel said to Zacharias—

Fear not, Zacharias: for thy prayer is heard; and thy wife Elizabeth shall bear thee a son, and thou shalt call his name John.

— Luke 1:13

—this being the son who would become John the Baptist, God made Zacharias dumb until his son was born. Why? Because God knew that Zacharias doubted whether this would really occur and that his doubtful word might abort the pregnancy in his wife's womb.

34

Distraction that allows doubt to seep in or pulls your mind away from attention on what you are trying to manifest will kill your vision. That is why it is so important to design your life so that once you are on the road to building what God has ordained, you can avoid things and people who will turn you aside from it. We will talk later in this chapter about what your friends indicate about you, and one of the key steps you must take in obeying the Laws of Thinking is removing friends from your life who will distract you from your goals.

You might be focused on building a business and getting rich, and they will come around talking about going out chasing women or hanging out with an old crowd that's into criminal activity. It is your *duty* to say no to such distractions; God expects it of you. After all, He's already at work manifesting what you have asked for! In Galatians 6:9, the King James Version says, *"And let us not be weary in well doing: for in due season we shall reap, if we faint not."* Every vision has its appointed time. Success never comes instantly; that's called winning the lottery, and your odds are one in a hundred million. Instead, be persistent in your focus and expel distraction from your life, and your season of reaping will *inevitably* come.

The Law of Attraction

By now, the Law of Attraction should be quite clear:

~

THE ENERGY THAT COMES OUT OF YOUR MIND WILL ATTRACT WHATEVER SUITS IT.

~

Your thoughts will shape your situation. They will direct your actions, determine the opportunities that come your way, and affect the outcome of the things you attempt. If you want to change your standing, you must change your thoughts. You must know the secrets of work—of magnetically imparting energy into action by focusing on purpose and forsaking distractions.

Do you know people who are negative thinkers and who lead unfulfilled lives of material want? Do you know people who expect disaster and are then stricken by disaster? There's a common phrase in English: "self-fulfilling prophecy." That is much truer than almost anyone realizes.

Prophecy is the interpretation of the Word of God. But that Word *is* reality; it is the Spirit that makes up everything that surrounds us as well as we ourselves. So interpreting the Word really means interpreting life: its events, signs and stages. A prophet brings blessing into your life by helping you decipher the meaning behind the Word that is inherent in every aspect of your life and discovering the good that God has spoken to you in that Word.

But when you lack the perspective of a prophet (and let's be honest, it is much easier for someone else to interpret the events of your life with the detached perspective of an outsider), it's easy to miss God's blessings and grace and become caught up in the negative.

~

YOU BECOME AN "ACCIDENTAL PROPHET" WITHOUT THE INSIGHT TO SEE THE GOOD IN WHAT IS COMING YOUR WAY, AND YOUR LIFE FULFILLS THE WANT AND LACK THAT EXISTS IN YOUR MIND.

~

We are all prophets receiving the Word of God, but very few can understand the multiple levels of meaning that the Word carries. That is why it is so vital to police your mind, to focus on moving upward, and to confidently declare your "I Am."

What Do Your Friends Say about You?

"Birds of a feather flock together." Ever hear that expression? Ever see a school cafeteria and see the jocks sitting with the jocks, the theater kids with the theater kids, and the gang kids all hanging out together? Like attracts like, and your thoughts will attract the kinds of people who will bring to fruition the thoughts you are having. Think prosperity and you will attract prosperous people; think poverty and you will attract those who are poor in Spirit as well as money.

Think prosperity and you will attract prosperous people . . .

If you watch the very successful, you will notice something: they attract a higher quality of person. When they have a new project in the works, quality people seem to come from nowhere with skills and resources that can help move that project along, and with the integrity and honor to keep their promises. That occurs because successful people have disciplined their minds to project thoughts of confidence, possibility, wealth and satisfaction. Those thoughts are like magnets for people of quality.

Friends are a prophecy of what you are becoming. If you're talking to millionaires, you're on your way to becoming one. When you want to change your life, get new friends. Associate with people who have what you want to have and who are what you want to become. Such people will serve your divine nature in many ways:

- They will be gateways to other people who can further your cause.

- They will teach you what they know about success, building a business, networking, and myriad other talents.

- You will "catch" the germ of their optimism, confidence and capacity for new ideas.

People of quality will attract more people of quality.

~

Quality people will become the "carriers" who "infect" you with the mindset of wealth and prosperity. When I associate with you, what's in you gets into me. I reproduce it. In this way, your associates shape your future.

Just as important, others will judge you by who you are seen with. People of quality will attract more people of quality. After all, if a busy millionaire is spending his precious time hanging out with you, you must be worth hanging out with!

The Whole Choir Goes to the Joint

Of course, every Law of God has an equal opposite side. If you hang out with people of low character, you will be associated with them. Your thoughts will begin to mirror their thoughts. Remember, people's thoughts and words are contagious; they can infect you with the germs of success as easily as failure.

Associate with people of poor quality and you become linked with them. In law enforcement, people who have nothing to do with a crime can get caught up and be arrested along with the rest. They were "in concert." They were accessories. The cops don't just arrest the soloist, but the whole choir! You are who you hang with! If you want to change your life, change your friends first. If it takes being brutal about it, be brutal.

Also, don't share your secret thought with lower powers, with people who are not prophets. Only share it with the power on high. Others will not understand.

God Sets in Motion, Then Sits Back and Watches

God will not argue with you; you will find no controversy in Him over how you are acting out His Word and expressing Spirit in this world. God isn't interested in debating you, but teaching you; He speaks and then backs off to see what you will do. In this way, He is truly a parent; just as all parents must do, He imparts His lessons and then lets go to see what will happen. He knows as all wise parents do that the best teacher is error and struggle, for only they lead to self-discovery. There is no right or wrong, there is only what serves the Spirit and what serves the flesh.

It's rather ironic given the debate between people who favor Creation or evolution, but God is really Darwinian. He believes in the survival of the spiritually fittest. God gives to you according to your faith. If you feel you are healthy, wealthy and wise, the Power on high will grant those things. If you feel you are dead, then you will be dead in Spirit until you can see otherwise. The Power on high is not concerned. What you ask for in Spirit shall be granted to you.

Be careful what you ask for. He who keeps asking, receives. He who keeps seeking, finds. For he who keeps knocking, the door will be opened.

What You Receive Will Be Without Form

We all have negative thoughts from time to time; it's an inevitable part of being human. So, does that mean that one stray thought will bring misfortune or a terrible person into your life? No. God doesn't work that way. Remember, everything is Spirit, so when God manifests something, it must always manifest as Spirit. The only way it can come into fleshly being is through Man.

Everything God creates will always be without form. When God brings something into your life, it will always begin without form, as a thought in the mind of God or in your own mind when you are in your "I Am" consciousness. That was how it was before Time, at the Creation: from the day God created man, he held man in his mind, and kept creating him. Just because something is not formed in flesh doesn't mean it's not formed in imagination.

What does that mean? You must keep that good thing you are creating in your mind and not let it go until the time is right for it to take form and shape. With the Law of Attraction, you will attract things and people to you that will make that idea in your mind manifest in reality. By the same token, if impoverished thoughts flit through your consciousness on occasion, you have nothing to worry about—as long as you do not dwell on those thoughts. As long as you do not make such thoughts habits, you will not manifest their negative consequences. It's persistent, focused thought that moves the invisible wheels of Spirit to bring new effects into your life.

That Check is Nonnegotiable

So the currency that pays for the blessings that manifest for you is your attention. What happens when God turns His attention to your life? You get a check from God, one that is nonnegotiable, brother. When God gives you a prophecy, you must hold it in your mind until you are ready to think it into form. You cannot negotiate your way out of it; you can only determine what that check will buy. But something will come into your life, and you must use your insight and Spirit to shape what it is.

Think about this:

~

WHAT YOU WILL CREATE IS RUNNING AROUND IN YOUR MIND, ALREADY CREATED.

~

God has created it in your mind and imagination already, and all He needs is you to be ready to bring it into manifestation. You will do that with your focus and attention, for good or ill. A prophetic word is the ass no man has ridden upon. It may be uncomfortable, but you must keep riding it until you are ready to think that prophecy into existence. Or it will throw you off!

To achieve the things God has ordained for you, you must always sow within as much as you sow without. If you don't go within, you are going to be without! While you are working in this world to bring your ideas and dreams into reality, always be working in the world of Spirit to obey God's Word and bring it into expression. Practice holding the image of what you want in your mind, without ceasing, until it comes into being. That's prayer without ceasing, experiencing God being god in *you*.

The truth is more than some people can handle, and exactly what others have been waiting for. The truth about prosperity is that what you want and desire is sitting within you, sleeping, waiting for you to wake it up. *Poverty is wealth asleep*. It is dormant within you. It is impossible for good to leave you. It is ready to

41

serve you when your mind, heart and spirit know that you love what you say you love.

* * *

SUMMARY

- Your purpose is to manifest the good of God.

- When you name something, you give it a nature.

- Focused attention is the currency that buys what you desire.

- Your thoughts will attract like things and people.

- We are all prophets, but most lack the skill to understand what they see.

- Your friends tell who you are and where you are going.

- God will not argue with you or debate you.

- The things that come into your life will first be without form.

- God's check is nonnegotiable.

Chapter 4

THE LAW OF WRITING

———✦———

Now that we've firmly established that manifesting the things God has ordained for your life is something that's in your control, we're going to talk about the ways you go about bringing forth that manifestation. But first, a few words about the misconception known as evil.

Evil is our favorite subject in church. We all like to talk about Satan doing this and Satan doing that, but the truth is that Satan is a convenient target for blame. There's a saying that goes, "Every time I've been stabbed in the back, I find my own fingerprints on the knife." Which means, most of the time when bad things happen in your life, it's because you thought, said or did something that caused them to manifest. Usually, the devil has nothing to do with it.

Here's something that will rock your world:

～

THERE IS NO SUCH THING AS EVIL.

～

There is only the lack of awareness of God. You create the only evil there is when you choose to walk a path that rejects the good in you and rejects the calling from God to express His Spirit in the world. When you lack the awareness of being god, you make everything impossible. When you're in that state, you can only be and not *become*. You are static. You begin to die years before your body gives out.

You are responsible for the divinity in your life, for using it, and for whether or not you miss the mark God has elected you to aim for. That mark is "I Am god," the awareness that frees your creative power to shape this reality.

> *When you lack the awareness of being god, you make everything impossible.*
>
> ∼

Writing Is the Key to Manifestation

Now we're going to talk about the power of writing. I have heard from several sources that when you speak about something—a goal, a plan, a business—you make it more likely to happen. But when you write about the same thing, you make it *five times* more likely to happen. Now, it would be easy to dismiss that as nothing more than the likelihood that when you write an idea you organize it, make lists of things to do, and develop it in a way you could not through speech. And that's true, but we know there is more to it than that. Writing turns out to be the key you can use to unlock those cosmic wheels and manifest the good things God has decreed you are to have in your life.

The importance of writing is talked about everywhere in the Bible. A few examples:

Then the Lord said to Moses, "Write this on a scroll as something to be remembered and make sure that Joshua hears it, because I will completely blot out the memory of Amalek from under heaven."

— Exodus 17:14

Then the LORD said to Moses, "Write down these words, for in accordance with these words I have made a covenant with you and with Israel."

— Exodus 34:27

"Speak to the Israelites and get twelve staffs from them, one from the leader of each of their ancestral tribes. Write the name of each man on his staff. On the staff of Levi write Aaron's name, for there must be one staff for the head of each ancestral tribe."

— Numbers 17:2-3

Let love and faithfulness never leave you; bind them around your neck, write them on the tablet of your heart.

— Proverbs 3:3

Writing Is Permanent

Writing is the first step in bringing your own intangible visions, callings and inspirations into three-dimensional, manifested form, while dissolving the fear of the future at the same time. Writing is a power source, a lasting form of expression that, even after you have stopped writing, continues to exist. Remember that the Word calls the thing forth, and the Word can be the thoughts of your mind or the speech of your mouth. Well, the Word can also be the product of your pen . . . or your computer keyboard. When you write down your thoughts or goals, positive or negative, they have a permanence that nothing else can match. That permanence is very much like the focused attention of your mind: it begins to bring forth things from the invisible and makes them start to manifest. Writing is a constant Word speaking into the Universe, 24/7. Even after you no longer hold the thought that fueled the writing in your mind, the written Word perpetuates it for better or worse. Writing carves your words in diamond!

Writing is like a covenant between you and God. Now, I'm not talking about writing out your grocery list or things like that. God does not care if you buy lowfat or nonfat milk. Let's not get ridiculous. But when you sit down to write out the things you desire or what you intend to create, that is making a pact with God. Since writing is not ephemeral like speech or thought, writing things down is similar to writing out a binding contract with the Creator. You are stating what you will do, and in return for your listening to His Word and acting to express His Spirit in the physical world, God promises as His part of the contract to bring forth the things you want from immaterial to material. It may take some time, but God always fulfills His part of the covenant.

The problem comes when you do not. Understand that when you speak or write the things you would like to manifest, God goes to work immediately bringing them into physical existence. He's not waiting to see if you'll pay your part of the vow: acting without doubt and in Spirit to manifest His design. He assumes you will. God trusts you as you trust Him. But when you fail to fulfill your part of the contract, God has to stop in the middle of His work to manifest through you. He won't punish you; God doesn't work that way. But by derailing the train that was bringing you closer to your goals, *you punish yourself.* You must wait that much longer for money, success or opportunity.

46

Writing Is Passport Control

You will notice that when you talk with highly successful people—people who have a habit of turning their ideas into manifested reality as companies, inventions or creative works—they are list makers. They write everything down. In part, it's because such people are very busy and need to record the creative energies of their brain in order to remember their ideas later on. But they also know the secret power of writing: that when you write down an idea, the mere act begins to prime the pump of creativity that resides in Spirit. Writing sets things in motion and begins to attract people, resources and money toward you.

In fact, writing plays a very precise role in the purpose of creation, which is to manifest, right? It's such an important role that I've called it the Law of Writing:

~

WRITING IS THE ENTRY POINT OF SPIRIT INTO MATTER.

~

As we have discussed, the purpose of Spirit is to express itself on the material plane. But because Spirit cannot become material itself, it must manifest through your mind and thoughts, using its power to eventually turn those thoughts into corporeal reality—money, houses, people, businesses. Well, it's only logical that as Spirit makes that transition from the ethereal realm to the material, there has to be a point of entry . . . a passport control station, if you will, where Spirit crosses into this world through you. That control station is the *written word*.

This is amazing and wonderful but true: each time you put pen to paper or fingers to keys to write out your ideas, dreams, plans, and goals, you are admitting Spirit into this realm. When you write the words, Spirit enters the physical world. It's as if your pen is the birth canal for Spirit and its intentions to be born on earth. Think about it: the angel Gabriel had to express a Word that Mary would give birth to a son, Jesus. That Word set the events in motion that would result in the incarnation of the Savior. When you sit down to write your future, you are doing exactly the same thing! That is why when I say you are god, I mean every word.

When you write the words, Spirit enters the physical world.

Writing powers the transition between the invisible and the visible. After you write something, you make it inevitable. Now, it may not come to pass in the way that you intend if you violate that covenant with God and get turned aside or distracted from your purpose. But *something* will happen once you set that machinery in motion. There's a saying, "Advertising never *doesn't* work." It always has an effect. When you write something, you set events in motion, and something is going to manifest. Whether it's what you want or not depends on you.

A Word about E-mail and the Internet

It's vital that our understanding of God and His purposes keep pace with the changes in human society and technology. That's why we have websites, streaming media, people participating in our teachings on prophecy in chat rooms around the world. But one thing we have not addressed yet with regard to the power of writing is the incredible power of e-mail and the Internet

The Internet is the most important tool for communication ever devised, and it's critical that you understand how the Net fits into the Law of Writing and your place in the goal of manifestation. Let's look at it like this: when you take a pad of paper and write down your intent to start a business, you are sharing it with one person, yourself. When you write it as a PowerPoint presentation and share it with 100 people in a meeting, you are multiplying the effect of writing by 100, because each of those people is a potential gateway to something that could manifest in your life to help you reach your goal. So what do you think happens when you send your business plans into the world via e-mail, where they can be forwarded to thousands of people, or when you post them on a website, where they can get picked up by the likes of Google and potentially seen by millions?

The more you circulate what you write, the more you multiply the power of writing to manifest change in your life. After all, careers and whole new industries have been created because people put their thoughts forth on the Internet for others to read using tools like weblogs. So what does this mean? It means that the more you use tools like e-mail and the Web, the more attention you must pay to what you write. Sending your thoughts out over such a global medium will bring strong changes into your life; what will determine if those changes help or hinder you is the nature of what you write. Write with creativity, passion, hope and invention and that is what you will receive. Send out vibes of hate, depression or distrust and that's what you will find not only in your Inbox, but in your life.

Writing Is the Gauge of Your Passion

If you cannot write your vision, you are not in earnest. If you can't write it, you don't really want it. We have discussed how focused attention is the key that unlocks the manifestation of the people, possessions and events that are promised to you. Based on that, it should be obvious that you need to keep your mind and your ideas as focused and consistent as possible. If you just think about your goals but never speak them or write them down, what's going to happen when you get busy with the flotsam of life, or when some difficulty comes along that pulls your focus from manifestation? You might forget some aspect of what you desire or set a goal that's different from what you first thought about.

But if you are truly committed to your goals, if your passion is true and you really want it more than anything, you'll write it down. When you write it, you force your mind to become more focused on steps, details, names, ideas. You set things in concrete. So write down your goals. Write down how much money you need to see every day. Keep writing greater goals. When you write, you wake up your mind. Its cells become active and go into the future to work on making matter of what is now only Spirit.

Your vision will not be a success until you can believe in it enough to put it on a billboard. You must put it out there so that people can see it in seconds, grasp it, and run and tell others. It must be plain and big so that everyone can see and understand it.

Grow in Dimensions of God

As we grow in Spirit, we grow in dimensions of God and learn to unlock all these ready treasures that the Universe has waiting for us. Some people never learn to write down their vision, so they never commit their minds to it and never call up the Spirit power that is waiting to express itself. Spirit is eager to be expressed; that is its purpose! So when you write down something that you want, you make it plain in your imagination and experience so it can play out and begin to develop. In a very real sense, you give Spirit a blueprint to work from in making that thing real for you!

You can do the same by cultivating the aspects of your spiritual self that are the various entry points of God into you. These go by various names, but in the Hindu faith they are called *chakras*. The seven chakras are energy centers for your body, focus points where the energy of Spirit both enters and leaves your body. As you learn this material and develop your ability to quiet your mind and ego and let yourself fully behold the Word of God, learn to perceive and control your chakras; they are like seven churches within you, each holding a different aspect of the Mystery of God.

These are the chakras:

1. First Chakra, called the Support Chakra. It resides in your pelvis, at the physical core of your body.

2. Second Chakra, the Self Chakra, It resides in your genital region and as you might expect, it channels energy related to family, procreation, and creativity.

3. Third Chakra, the Navel Chakra. It should be obvious where this one resides: in your solar plexus at the base of your spine, the center of your movement. It directs energy related to ego, the desire for power and the need for advancement. This is an important chakra to manage and understand.

4. Fourth Chakra, the Heart Chakra. This chakra resides near your heart, and it channels energy related to devotion, self-confidence and selfless service.

5. Fifth Chakra, the Throat Chakra. This one lives in the area of the neck that corresponds to the cervical spine. This is the knowledge chakra, responsible for directing energy toward intellect, spiritual awareness, and simple living.

6. Sixth Chakra, the Third Eye Chakra. This chakra resides between your eyebrows and is the spiritual catalyst of self-awareness.

7. Seventh Chakra, the Crown Chakra. This chakra resides at the top of your cranium, and it focuses energies on oneness with all things. If you are to be one with God, you must develop this chakra.

Talk about chakras, a principle from a non-Christian faith, may be shocking to some. But this teaching is really nothing more than the Hindu version of an essential cosmic truth that defies religious doctrine: God has entry points into your Spirit just as He does into this world. Whether you call it a chakra or something completely different, the truth of the idea remains. God is always looking for ways to work through you, and these spiritual gateways allow Him to speak to various aspects of your self, to deliver grace, revelation and anointing. Get past doctrine and understand how these manifestation points work and what they do for you.

History Is Written Down, Why Not Future?

In the realm of Spirit, time means nothing. Yesterday, today and tomorrow exist side by side, and God can see all things that have transpired and those that have yet to transpire in our consciousness. When you accept that you are Spirit, then think about the power of writing in that context. Writing something down finalizes it, makes it concrete. History is written down in the decrees of kings and the lines of founding documents. But if time means nothing, why not write down your future history? The past exists in the minds of men and the words on documents, but your future exists the same way. When you write it, you reach into the future and set events and things in motion. You become your own future historian! With the thing written down, it becomes far easier for you to achieve that future; all you need to do is knit the two ends—the now and the future that your writing has already declared—together!

What You Want Is Already Out There

Writing is the gateway to what you wish to receive. If you are in earnest about something, write it. Decide to give yourself permission to have and receive what you love. *What you desire is out there already, waiting for you to declare that you are that thing, so it can begin to manifest!* Your thoughts, tongue and hands must become a pen of the ready writer.

* * *

SUMMARY

- There is no such thing as evil.
- Writing is the key to manifestation.
- Writing is thought made permanent.
- Writing is the entry point for Spirit into matter.
- The Internet multiplies the power of your writing.
- Chakras are the entry points for God's Spirit into you.
- You are your own future historian.

Chapter 5

THE LAW OF RISK

‒‒‒•◦•‒‒‒

God is a God of potential, not of actuality. That's heavy, so I'll explain what it means. God does ordain something that you will have; he ordains something that you can achieve, but you have to walk the path to achieving it. God will never place something in your hands. He will only share with you the information you need to know to go and get it yourself!

The key to unlocking that potential is prophecy. Without prophecy, potential remains dormant. God reveals His secrets to prophets. Without prophecy, you are asleep to your potential. You see, prophets operate in spiritual manifestation, while you are operating in dense flesh. Prophecy sees beyond the material into the timeless realm of Spirit and discerns the meaning behind the Word of God. You must understand: that which God has created from the beginning is never seen in the now, only in the Spirit. Spirit will tell you what can be, but until you gain the ability to quiet your mind and let God speak to you, that information must come to you via prophecy. The prophetic word pronounces the mystical unseen nature of Spirit.

Why should you want that information? Here's the astonishing reason:

CREATION IS WAITING FOR YOU TO MANIFEST.

Isn't that amazing? Creation is waiting for you—for all of us—to declare "I Am the house, the car, the bank account" so it can open up its vault of riches and bring you the things you desire most. You are God's proxy on this earth, His physical expression of Himself, and Creation is yours to command—if you know the keys to unlock that vault!

God . . . the Liar?

Now we begin to get to the crux of this chapter. God always speaks truth when He talks to you about what Spirit has in store for you. However, when your perception is grounded in the mundane world of the flesh, whatever God says to you will look like a lie. That's a crucial idea, so let's repeat it:

WHATEVER GOD SPEAKS TO YOU AT FIRST WILL LOOK LIKE A LIE.

That's because it only exists in Spirit and has yet to press itself out into manifestation. You cannot see the truth of God until you write the vision and see in Spirit. God might say to you—either directly or through a prophet—"You are a successful movie producer with a mansion and a house in Italy and you travel on a private jet." And you might look around and say, "Um, Lord, I don't know if you've taken a look but I live in a three-room apartment and I don't have two nickels to rub together." And God will say, "No, that's what you are."

Now, you might think God is pulling your leg, but that's because you're operating in the world of the material. In the world of Spirit, you already are those things, and it is a matter of persistent focus, effort and mental energy to bring those things in spiritual existence into manifestation in your physical consciousness. The external should never be your reality; only the internal should be. So while you are mired in the material, yes, God will look like a liar. But that's because to reach the point where you can honestly say, "Yes, I AM that house, that career, that bank account," you must make a leap to the Spirit. And that leap is what God's favor is all about.

> *The external should never be your reality; only the internal should be.*
>
>

Want Is Hell

In the Christian faith, there's a lot of talk about Hell. But I'm asking you to forget about your old notions of Hell, because they're simply not valid. Instead, it's time to embrace a new truth: *want is hell.* When you "want," it is not just because you do not have. Want indicates that you do not *understand*—understand God's system and how He operates. Without that understanding, you cannot hope to achieve the wonderful things God has in mind for you. And what is Hell but the absence of hope?

When you operate in Spirit to make your thoughts manifest, you cannot know want, because want is covetousness—it is an indication that you know you will never have what it is you desire. Fear and guilt are traps. You must live boldly, fearlessly, or you will live a life of want. But when you are working in Spirit, you cannot want, because you know that if you think it, and then pursue it persistently and tirelessly in Spirit, it will come. There is no want where there is understanding of how God works. There is fulfillment in the realm of the Spirit, which inevitably leads to fulfillment in the material realm. But you must first feel that what you want already exists—you must *know* that you are the things you desire. From "full-feel-ment" comes fulfillment. When you can do that, want will be banished from your consciousness.

You Are Not a Slave to a Wage

Want has another toxic side: it makes you believe that you must battle uphill, with the sweat of your brow, to achieve even a tiny part of your birthright. Want implies that you do not believe you *deserve* that which you desire. You do. You deserve everything God has ordained for you, or He would not have ordained it! Want makes you a slave, and if you understand nothing else from this chapter, understand this:

~

YOU ARE NOT A SLAVE TO A WAGE.

~

When you find the purpose and passion that allow you to let go of ego and act in the confidence of "I Am," you will find motivation, people who will help you, and success from within to without. Success is not 10% inspiration and 90% perspiration, as the saying goes. It is the other way around. That's why poverty stinks. The poor work with their hands; they are slaves to a wage because they create nothing. You are a Creator, co-equal with God. Act like it!

Prophets don't sweat. Making a living with the sweat of your brow is the curse of Adam. Young people are supposed to sweat and work, because they are learning. But when you're older and you come fully into your awareness of Spirit and how God operates in this world, you should be using the power of your mind to make money. Inspiration, ideas, vision and Spirit will make you wealthy. The work of your body will only make you sweat and make you poor. Ideas create wealth; slavery destroys health.

God is not sweating in heaven. Why? He's a Creator. He intends for you to do the same—to build a manifestation of prosperity and of giving back to Him, His church and others using your ideas, your innovation, your inspiration, your dreams and your artistry. Who are the people who are the super-rich among us? Those who create things: companies, technologies, music, books, films, inventions. No one ever became prosperous pushing a lawn mower or repairing plumbing. You can make a living doing those things, but you cannot get rich and change the world. Money is the force of change in this world, and you will never have enough money to change things if you are a wage slave. You have the option not to be one, so start today to earn the wages your mind pays you! What ideas do you have that could make you prosperous?

God Challenges You

It all seems so complicated, doesn't it? You begin to glimpse the truth: God has made these Laws complex for a reason: challenging us to go beyond the simple is the way He gets us to perceive this world in a different way—the right way. The reason we have challenges is because we do not see that everything that is or occurs is the product and the work of God. Everything operates according to the Laws that He has set down.

So your problems are a matter of your misperception of the situation, not real problems at all. Misfortunes or lack of opportunity are merely you misperceiving the true nature of the forces God is trying to manifest in your life. He doesn't put things in your hands; He sets the path before you and you have to walk it. Challenges are God's way of motivating us to expand our minds, change our perceptions and develop our Spirits. Challenge is God's way of calling you to stretch, risk and push your limits. When you have no challenges, you feel miserable, because challenge is purpose. You must have challenge, purpose and risk or you are not alive.

Challenges are God's way of motivating us to expand our minds, change our perceptions and develop our Spirits.

When you are in your "I Am" state, you will find that you have formed every problem, and that you are the solution. As it says in Genesis, God formed all the beasts of the world. God also formed all your situations, but you have the power to perceive them as problems or challenges or opportunities. How you perceive them will determine how they manifest in the physical world. What you call it determines whether you ride the beast or the beast rides you! You already know how to rope the beast; whatever comes to you, if you name it good, it is good. If you name it bad, it will be bad. You can take that beast and name it expansion or opportunity. Count it all joy!

Is this fair? Why not? If every time you asked for something it fell in your lap, you would not learn to work. If every time you shot the ball, it went in, you would have no motivation to improve. God takes no pleasure in making things too easy for you; you must learn and grow stronger in faith and imagination. God is our Father, and like any parent, He wants His children to learn on their own to be stronger and wiser. If that means a few stumbles along the way, then the lessons will last longer.

The Catalyst

Now we come to the heart of this chapter, and to one of the most important concepts in the realm of human beings creating or building anything of worth. I've told you that the Laws of Thinking operate in much the same way as the laws of nature. Well, in chemistry, there are constant chemical reactions that make things happen. Your body is full of chemical reactions that are turning food into energy, making your brain and nervous system function, and so on. But every reaction must have a catalyst, something that gets it started. The same is true for the Laws of Thinking. To create great things and to manifest that which God intends for you, you need a catalyst. You need to make things happen. That catalyst is RISK.

Here's a bit about the mind of God: You can't draw back from a breakthrough situation that takes you out of your comfort zone. God only has pleasure when you're leaning in. If you want God to have pleasure in you, you've got to stretch yourself thin. You must strive, test and dare the jaws of the lion. Ease offers God nothing. You must always grow. You must always be overcoming your fear—*becoming* fearless. Many of us are running from a roar, and there's no bite in the lion making the roar! We've been taught that risk is bad, but risk is the key to success! This is the Law of Risk:

61

YOU WILL NEVER ACHIEVE GREAT THINGS WITHOUT GOING OUT ON THE EDGE AND RISKING.

Risk is God's catalyst. It is the force that wakes Spirit up and makes it say, "All right, now I've got something to work with!" Getting out of your comfortable space, doing what terrifies you in spite of the fear tells God that you are not letting your intellectual doubts get in the way of your 100% confidence that God will make good things happen.

You need to live a life of faith, never pausing or hesitating. You need to jump knowing there's going to be a net there. You need to set in motion what takes lots of money even though you don't have an extra dollar in your pocket. Risk is about action, not consideration.

Live a Life of Risk

When you live this way, you will never arrive. You will always walk through the never-ending seasons. You must always go forward—not worrying about things, living in God, doing—knowing that faith will bring what you need.

You see, God only gets pleasure when He is believed. Doubt is the greatest sin! Don't wait for God to give you an umbrella—He needs you to go out into the rain without doubt and know that sunshine will appear. Only by doing that will you catalyze the reactions that will begin to manifest what God needs you to manifest. You must run heedless, hanging over the edge at all times, believing that God is all you need and God is within you. You must *know* you *are* god!

God takes no pleasure with you in safety. He only works for you when you are on the edge. That's why He keeps knocking you out of that safety zone. You must be stretched if you are going to develop your talents, your ideas and your perceptions. You will never, ever get rich without a risk. You've got to get out where the action is.

God in you is opportunistic. He is always looking to be expressed, looking for another miracle to pull off, looking to prove that the supernatural outweighs the natural. That's why you should never fear risk. People who are fully realized in Spirit actually go toward risk when they see it, because they know something amazing:

~

RISK IS JUST "OPPORTUNITY" MISSPELLED.

~

Going into debt, starting a new art form, these are all risks. But let me tell you something: God only rewards originality. He is a Creator, and only rewards true creativity. The world rewards difference, not sameness. Have you ever read a front-page story about some famous author or explorer that said, "He copied ideas from everyone around him?" Of course not! We revile people who steal the works of others. But we reward those who take audacious risks, endure being called heretics or fools, and turn that risk into an incredible new addition to human culture. Nobody ever celebrated a man who played it safe.

Debt is proof that you are a risk taker—that you live in a place where God has pleasure in you because you are stretching yourself. The only people who are out of debt are in the grave. Rap music was one of the most at-risk art forms ever created; now it's a huge cultural force. Prince, Kanye West . . . the world is full of people who took risks, were told, "You can't do that," and have had the last laugh. They knew that playing it safe is the last step before being in the grave. You must believe in your passions and trust the voice from God that tells you to go ahead. God only takes pleasure in those who are at risk.

> *. . . when you take a risk and others tell you you're crazy or a heretic, smile.*
>
>

Every Messiah Is a Risk

Jesus' birth was a risk to him and to society, because he was the threat of overturning that societal order; that's why he was killed. The clearest sign that Jesus was on the right path to doing God's will was when he was reviled. Let me tell you, when you take a risk and others tell you you're crazy or a heretic, smile. Every hero is someone's heretic, and every terrorist is someone's deliverer. It means you're out there, stretching and infuriating the folks whose only interest is preserving the status quo. You must not pull back from controversy. You must lean into it. If you have controversy, and you have followed your vision and the passion that comes from your Spirit, you cannot fail if you follow through on your risk. Here's another bit of wisdom:

YOU MUST KEEP YOURSELF IN THE "EMERGENCY ZONE," OR YOU WILL NOT "EMERGE."

When God calls you to do something, you're going to see His other side. The same one who's bringing you the vision is making things harder for you. That's because God only has pleasure when you are at risk, when you are struggling to break out of a hard place. You have to be able to walk out in the middle of traffic and count your victory. Risk takers make the news. You only get noticed when you take a risk. If you don't take a risk, you're not going to get paid. If you don't go out on the limb, you're not going to get the fruit.

When you're living fully in God's Laws, you will always walk the high wire. You will live stretched, never arriving. Even when you're a millionaire, you will not have arrived. You must always be in debt, always be stretching, always be taking risks and risking disaster. When you reach one goal, you'll start running toward five new ones that are even farther away.

Nothing Worthwhile Comes Without Struggle

This is life. If a child did not take the crown of his head and break the water sac of his mother and draw blood, he would not be born. Nothing worthwhile comes without struggle. The poor don't understand this, which is why they're out of the game of life. They don't get the 80/20 Rule:

$\sim$

80% OF PEOPLE MAKE 20% OF THE MONEY, 20% OF THE PEOPLE MAKE 80% OF THE MONEY.

$\sim$

The 20% who make the money take 100% of the risk. Unless you're daring, you will get no action or money. Everyone who runs with the herd goes over the cliff.

Everything in life is at risk. The problem comes when you put a value on what you are risking and you let that determine your level of joy and your life's actions. Let God worry about the value;

just go after the risk. If you seek to keep your life, you lose it. If you play it safe, you will not live. Seek to risk everything; you will live and live beautifully.

Proverbs says, "There is that scattereth, reap." If you throw it out there, you will gain. If you hold back and play it safe, you will reap nothing. More important, others will have control over what you reap! When you try to save money, it puts you in want. When you scatter it, it comes back to you. When you give God all that you are, He can be all He can be within you.

Every Savior Needs a Devil

Take a screenwriting class sometime and one of the first principles you'll learn is that there is one element that is central to drama. It's not story, character or dialogue. What is it?

〰️

CONFLICT.

〰️

There is no drama without conflict: people striving against opposition to reach important goals with a great deal at stake. Stakes, opposition, challenge goals—these are the essence of story.

In the same way, the story of life is conflict. God places adversaries and obstacles in your path because He knows your nature. After all, He created you, and your nature is His nature! God needs challenges, and you are His challenge. And He knows that overcoming adversity is what makes us all grow, develop, find wisdom and realize our potential.

Every savior needs a devil. Life is conflict. Life needs opposites. You are trying to write the story of your life, and there is no story without conflict. Without opposition, problems and adversaries, your existence has no meaning. You need problems and opponents in order to live and fulfill your purpose. If you don't have one, take a risk and create one! Risk creates the opponents and obstacles that we all need in order to have purpose.

How powerful is that? Rather than avoiding risk, you should go out and seek risk to give yourself the purpose that defines your life! Go out and create new businesses, try crazy new ventures, do something that other people tell you can't be done, and stick your neck out. It's the only way you'll see what's in your future.

Find Your Love and Ignore the Professionals

How do you know what constitutes a smart risk for you? Find what you *love*. Go deep inside yourself and listen to that passion that speaks from God in your gut. Find what you were meant to do, no matter what it is. That is your purpose. If you don't, you will hate what you aren't doing. You must open yourself to giving and receiving what you love.

But a warning: when you start moving in the Spirit and taking bold risks, you must be watchful for people advising you who are not moving in the Spirit. Do not follow their advice, for they will tell you what *cannot* be done.

What I call "professionals" will put you outside the Spirit, because all they can see is material made of limitations. They deal in limits, and only the Spirit is limitless. There's always an abortion clinic telling you, you can abort this vision right now. Fear is always waiting to try and derail your vision from manifesting. You will always have a choice: abort or wait for birth. The bearers of fear will always be there to whisper in your ear and tell you it's impossible. Professionals will steer you away from the mind of God.

I heard a story about a student who was assigned to write a paper about his dream. He wrote a paper about his dream to own horses. His teacher gave him an F and told him his dream was unrealistic and to write about a more realistic dream. He told her, "You keep your F. I'll keep my dream." Now he owns a 160-acre ranch raising horses! Dreams shape reality, but only if you refuse to let the professional dream-exterminators kill yours.

Find your dream! Make it happen and do not let yourself be dissuaded by professionals. God put that passion into you, and that is where you will find your fullest expression.

* * *

SUMMARY

- Creation is waiting for you to manifest.

- What God speaks to you will look like a lie at first.

- Want is Hell.

- You are not a slave to a wage.

- God will always challenge you.

- Risk is the catalyst for wealth in your life.

- God is only pleased when you hang out on the edge and risk.

- God places adversaries and obstacles in your path.

- If you find your love, you find your purpose.

Chapter 6

THE LAW OF HABIT

———•◦•———

In this chapter, we're going to take a look at the habits that define and channel your actions. To begin, let's look at the habit of guilt. Guilt is like fear: it has no useful purpose. Guilt is you misleading yourself that the past could have been anything other than what it was. Guilt traps you in the past, and you want to be moving forward into the future that God has decreed for you.

You must learn to let go of guilt if you are to work in Spirit and express God's design in your life. Guilt is one of the great distractions: it pulls your mind from its focus on your desire and makes you ashamed of something that you cannot change. To release guilt when you feel it, try some of these steps:

- Write about it.

- Talk to someone about it.

- Meditate about it.

Any of these actions will dissolve the guilt and free you from its prison. But if you are to be fully realized as "I Am," you must

THE LAWS OF THINKING

eventually adopt the habit of living without guilt, just as you must live without fear. So when you feel guilt over your past, just remind yourself, "That was a different person. I was not working in Spirit as I am now." Spirit gives you the power to redeem that guilt just as Jesus redeemed your soul.

Recognize Your True Self

In the end, you are a complex being, a perfect reflection of the Father. You have many aspects—mind, spirit, personality, ego, body and so on. Before you can manifest, you must come to understand your various selves and recognize which ones are real and which are either created by fear and guilt or are counterproductive, such as ego. Recognizing your true self clears the way for Spirit to come through you and manifest. Much of your work is clearing the baggage of those other selves, finishing unfinished business, putting it to rest.

. . . you are a complex being, a perfect reflection of the Father.

It's as if you are clearing debris out of the road from the incorporeal world of the Spirit to the material life you are living. The clearer you make the road, the more things Spirit can send toward you to make your thoughts manifest. Eventually, your goal is to be a fully realized Spirit-being, a co-creator with God whose physical body is just a wonderful tool to be used to manifest. All your other selves must be subordinate to that self.

All this talk of you being co-equal with God and all may tempt you to feel arrogant, and arrogance may make you feel sinful. Nonsense. We will talk later in this book about the importance of humility before God, but that doesn't mean you must be humble before your fellows. Being the vessel of the Lord and His Spirit is an exalted state; you are right to feel blessed and superior to some others. It is okay to feel a little arrogance.

Some people think it pleases God when they're feeling guilty and humble. They believe that it's arrogant to be confident and walk strong. But who is more arrogant than God? He created the Universe, for pity's sake! You don't think He sits back on His throne once in a while, folds His arms and says, "Yeah, I did all right"? Of course he does! There's nothing wrong with acknowledging your higher state. Just don't become obnoxious about it.

God's People Will Give You What You Need

Here's a basic, core principle to learn:

~

GOD WILL NEVER GIVE YOU ANYTHING THAT YOU DON'T NEED.

~

That means when people or things arrive in your life and bring you things that take you away from your destiny as "I Am," they are not from God. God never sends forces into your life unless they advance your cause. Now, it's up to you to recognize those forces for what they are, and if you don't, that's just too bad. But good will always come from God.

This knowledge is perfect for vetting the people who enter and pass through your life. People can do much to enhance your progress toward wealth and prosperity, or they can be a hurricane that will wreck the palace you are building. God will only send people into your sphere of influence who will bring blessings. Here's an example: God will never give a woman a man she can control. God will never give a man a woman who is not submissive. The equation is simple, but people like to entertain the distraction. If a woman has more money than the man, she can control him. Man was meant to be in control; woman to be his helpmate.

People who defy the roles in life that God has designed will bring you low! They will waste your money, turn aside your good fortune and distract you from the good you are trying to do. Learn and live by this fact:

~

ANYONE IN YOUR LIFE WHO CANNOT GIVE YOU WHAT YOU NEED—MONEY, SUPPORT, SHELTER—IS NOT SENT BY GOD. THAT PERSON IS SENT BY HELL TO DERAIL YOU FROM YOUR PURPOSE.

~

You must understand *assignments*. People are either assigned by Heaven or Hell. Learn to know which one!

Your Life Practice

What does a doctor do? He practices. What does a lawyer do? He *practices*. People practice things to become more proficient at them. As part of his practice, is a doctor required to continue learning? Of course! If he doesn't continually expand his medical knowledge, he doesn't get to keep his license to practice. Life is exactly the same way. We should practice every day to become more adept at listening to, understanding and acting on the Word of God.

Practice by its very nature implies what? That you are maintaining a persistent focus on your goal. And that, as we have already discussed, is the key to manifestation. Here's a huge thought: you are only on earth for practice. Everything you do is to get ready for a greater performance, because you don't know which performance is going to be the one that's going to take you over the edge. You must always be getting better in order to be ready for the "tipping point," when everything God has been setting aside for you fully manifests. Some people miss the fun in life because they hate practicing.

When you send out certain vibrations, certain results will come to you.

Practice is more than a way of working on your skills, talents, and above all, your ability to listen to God. It's also a way of sending out vibrations that say, "I'm searching for what I am meant for." When you send out certain vibrations, certain results will come to you. You don't make music; music finds you. Eventually, with enough practice, what you are looking for will find you. You become attuned to *capturing* Spirit.

It's difficult to get what you want without practice, but practicing is challenging, because you must do it daily even if that day doesn't bring your breakthrough. Most days don't, but that doesn't absolve you of your responsibility to practice. How do you build muscle at the gym? You lift weights every day, a little more each week, and slowly your muscles grow. That's the diligence required for practicing the life you want to have. Some basketball players never get into the game, but they have to be at practice.

Proverbs talks about diligence, consistently doing something over and over again and again, repeating it until it is completely inside you. That is what you must begin doing: declaring yourself to be "I Am" every day and becoming the things you want, practicing that kind of confidence and fearless action daily until what you want begins to manifest. Practice does not make perfect, it makes better. You will never reach perfect, and you should never hope to. You should always *aspire*.

The Law of Habit

What we're really talking about are habits. Habits are like little machines that run inside your brain that make you do the same things, at the same time, in the same way. You may not think you are controlled by your habits, but the Law of Habit says otherwise:

$\sim$

YOU *ARE* YOUR HABITS.

$\sim$

Your habits can rob you of your conscious will to control your actions and lead you to actions that are not in the interest of your partnership with God. True spirituality should be a realignment of the soul. What are your habits? Habits create destiny. What do you do religiously? Your habits are your religion, because they will determine where you end up.

Habits create success. Successful people have "success habits." Why do you think there is a mega-bestselling book called *The 7 Habits of Highly Successful People*? Because multi-millionaires know that if you can adjust your mental and physical habits to direct you to do the things that serve God's purpose and your own goals, you will move toward success on autopilot. Your habits will create your position in life.

By the same token, bad habits will destroy your hopes. How many men and women with so much potential for so much good have gotten out of prison with high hopes, only to be sent into a personal Hell because they could not break the habit of consorting with the people who got them into drugs or crime in the first place? Drug abuse, after all, is called a "habit." Do you have the habit of telling yourself that you can't do something because the money isn't there, when what you should be doing is jumping and knowing that God will provide the money when it's needed? That's a destructive habit. Putting yourself on that kind of autopilot steers you away from God and leads to a life of misery. The word *malpractice* simply means the practice of bad habits.

Experts say that it takes three months of daily repetition of an action to create new nerve pathways in the brain and turn something into a habit. Do you think you can trust God and take passionate, persistent action according to His will every day for only 90 days? I certainly hope you can, or you're reading the wrong book. But I will make you a promise:

∼

IF YOU CAN ADOPT HABITS THAT SERVE GOD,
YOU WILL MASTER THE LAWS OF THINKING.

∼

You will become so good at whatever you do that manifestation will become automatic. It will become instinct, with no filtering of the Spirit. The right habits create the right destiny; the wrong habits create the wrong destiny. For you, which habits are which?

Life Is about Fun

One of the most common misperceptions I see when I talk to people about operating in Spirit and serving God is that life will be a grind of constant demands from the Lord. Nothing could be further from the truth! God wants you to take joy in life! Life and love are the same thing; God created life out of love. You were meant to take joy in each day, to live from your passion and do the things that make every day a blessing. Do you think God put all that work into Creation because it was drudgery? Creating should be joyous!

Life is about joy and fun. "Function" means fun plus unction, which means ceremony. If you're not enjoying life, you need more fun in your unction. You need to do what you love and not worry about the money. When you do, every day is giving glory to the Lord—that's the unction.

God wants you to take joy in life!

~

You should always be journeying, finding new wonders, new delights. When you're having fun, there is no top to reach. You never arrive—you always journey. You are always growing and finding new things to manifest, new ways to create and give. You never come to rest. There is always a horizon to steer for. Fully realize who you are and just follow your passion and purpose! Trust what you feel!

Giving Will Make You Wealthy

There is so much joy to be had, and nothing creates more joy than giving. Work is not about living, but about giving. Work will never make you a millionaire. You will become one by creating and inspiring with your vision and your ideas.

How do you become prosperous? Practice—giving, sowing seeds, accepting no shortcuts. Practice, practice, practice. Always be doing more: give more, work more, study more, and grow more.

Practice giving and you will practice receiving. Giving selflessly makes you more like Christ!

The Four Questions

Finally, I want to leave this chapter by giving you four questions you should ask yourself at this stage of the book, questions that will help you determine what you have learned. These are HOTs, or Higher Order Thinking questions, and they will propel you to the next stage of awareness and thus to the next stage of life. Answering them will help you find your purpose. The questions: positive outcomes into your life, or if they are there to hinder you.

1. **Where did I come from?**

2. **Why am I here now?**

3. **Where am I going?**

4. **Who am I?**

The four questions are also a mantra that helps you stay focused and brings you back from the things or people that might distract you. They remind you of your mission. Ask yourself the questions now and spend some time mulling over your answers.

The questions have another purpose: you can ask them of anyone who comes into your life to see if they are there to serve your purpose, help you develop good habits and bring blessings to you, or to turn you aside from your goals? If someone wants to come into your life, ask them these four questions. Do they know the answers? These questions can only be answered by someone who is fully aware in Spirit and understands his or her habits, purpose, goals and strengths. If the person cannot answer, they are not from God. And if they are not there to enhance and unlock an aspect of your purpose, then they do not belong with you.

SUMMARY

- God doesn't give you anything you don't need.

- People who don't give you what you need are from Hell.

- You must practice at life.

- You are your habits.

- Life should be fun and joyous; you need fun in your unction.

- You will get wealthy by giving.

- Ask the Four Questions.

Chapter 7

THE LAW OF PASSION

———————

It's vital to stay on course toward what you wish to manifest. Present distractions prevent coming attractions. All you have to do is get off the path, get caught up in someone else's drama, and you can lose the great thing you were trying to accomplish. That's why you must take great care to associate only with people who bring positive energy, ideas, encouragement and integrity into your life—people who are treading the same upward path as you are, toward God and a greater self.

How exhausting is it for you to deal with someone else's drama? How much time have you wasted in your life listening to someone else's sob story when what you really wanted to do was give them a swift kick in the backside and tell them to grow up and start figuring things out? People who are not enlightened, who do not understand what it means to listen to God and act with the fearlessness and sense of mission that it takes to bring Spirit into being, will suck energy from you. They will become albatrosses around your neck, as in the great Samuel Taylor Coleridge poem, "The

Rime of the Ancient Mariner." Distance yourself from such people, for they are the worst kind of distraction; they can pull you into their orbit and waste your time. They are black holes.

JOB = Just Over Broke

In this chapter, we're going to talk at great length about following your passion and finding your sense of purpose, but before we do, we need to address some of the factors that limit us and prevent us from doing the things we should be able to do. To cut to the chase, we're talking about money and your perception of it.

When people look at money, what they usually perceive is *scarcity*—the lack of money. Their concern in doing anything is "What is this going to cost me?" when it should be "What am I going to make from this?" They are already thinking about losing money, and as we have seen, your thoughts shape the outcome, and if you try to keep something you lose it. When your main concern is about conserving your money instead of putting it out there and letting it dance at work for you, you've already guaranteed defeat.

Ask yourself: how many people do you know who have talked about starting their own business of some kind, from a bakery to an Internet company? How many do you know who have been talking about such a thing for years, but never done it? After a while, you're tempted to say, "Either do it, or stop yapping about it!" Deep down, these people know the truth about money and prosperity: you will never get rich at a job. You only become wealthy when you create something—when you slip the bonds of a job and take control of your earning potential.

A job gives someone else control over your power to create. Money is the creative power of God made manifest; never let anyone tell you anything different. There is no contradiction between

80

God and money. Money is god. (We'll talk more about this in a later chapter.) At a job, you might get paid by the week, but it can also be spelled "weak." If you're basing your pay on a week's salary, you are a weak person. Your wage should be daily bread, not the money someone else is deciding you are worth! Let me tell you this:

∼

GOD HAS ALREADY DECIDED WHAT YOUR WORTH IS.

∼

Why would you give someone else control over what you can achieve? Those who talk about starting a business but never do it have one thing in common: fear. They fear failure, so they never get started. Fear is just another way of saying you don't trust God enough to stick your neck out and lean into the risk. A job is nothing more than training wheels—you learn to get up, go to lunch and come back on time, do your job, etc. It's a prison. You can't be an entrepreneur unless you have the discipline to handle a business and money, and you will never learn to do that until you can leave the security of a job.

Cowering in the false security of a job means that you are limited to what your salary will allow you to do. That's the hidden meaning of the word *allowance*: it's what your money will allow you to do. Instead of spending the currency of your Spirit, you are limiting yourself by only seeing the paper currency you have in front of you. Your money should not have the power to allow you to do anything! Learn and remember this truth:

∼

AS LONG AS YOU KEEP TO A JOB, YOU WILL ONLY MAKE OTHERS RICH.

∼

God Wants You to Have a Gulfstream Jet

People mistakenly think God wants His true followers to live in poverty, as if there is some virtue to poverty. Nothing could be further from the truth. The Bible does not say money is evil; it says that the *love* of money is the root of all evil. If you are creating your wealth through God's system and man-ifesting things that serve Him and also create prosperity for others, you are acting exactly as He wants you to act.

Money is not everything; freedom is.

What God wants you to have more than anything else is *freedom*: the free-dom to act to express that which Spirit wants to express through you, the freedom to follow your passions to their conclusion, and the free-dom to create a life of joy, fun, fulfillment and giving back to others. Money is not everything; freedom is. But you cannot have freedom until you have money. Even people who say they have renounced material possessions completely and gone to live in a sod hut in the forest and meditate are not free, because they must spend much of their time on simple survival. They may lead an existence that fulfills them, but they will never lead an existence that fulfills God.

God wants you to *produce*. God wants you to prosper within his system. He wants you to have a Gulfstream jet, a fine car and a fantastic home, because when you have those things, you have enough money to cause change to happen in the world. Look at Bill Gates. He's the world's richest man, and one benefit of that is that through his foundation he has given millions of dollars to help end the AIDS scourge in Africa. That would not be possible if he was toiling in a computer repair shop in Seattle.

Freedom is the freedom to choose to be rich, to choose the path that will create prosperity. The difference between rich and poor is that the rich have choices, while the poor do not. The rich make choices every hour of every day, the poor have no choices.

You have start thinking like an *entrepreneur* if you are to have real freedom. There are three types of people in this world:

1. Technicians

2. Managers

3. Entrepreneurs

Technicians are nothing more than skilled labor, whether the labor is mowing grass or piloting an airliner. Managers direct the actions of technicians, but they create nothing. They control the worker bees, but they remain bees. Entrepreneurs are the ones who strategize, create companies, find funding, start businesses, and execute vision. Entrepreneurs spend their lives taking risks, which makes them favorites of God. Remember, He is pleased when people go out on a limb, dare the odds, and make things happen!

Successful people are entrepreneurs. You should work on your business, not in your business. If you are an entrepreneur, don't manage your business. If you do, you will be bogged down in details. Entrepreneurs hire managers to handle day-to-day details, and those managers hire the technicians that do the work that make the entrepreneurs rich. Entrepreneurs are all about scale—grand ideas, big visions, huge dollars, massive goals. They build skyscrapers, islands, bridges and cities. And you'll notice, even though the technicians are doing the work, they are not determining their own worth. God may know what they are worth, but:

GOD WILL NOT GIVE YOU WHAT YOU'RE WORTH.
YOU MUST PAY YOURSELF.

If you are a technician, no matter how skilled, you will never pay yourself what God knows you are worth. Only becoming an entrepreneur allows you to do that. Work your mind, not your behind!

Passion Is Profitable

At the center of every one of us, buried deep within our Spirit, is some calling. It's something we would do for no money, something we can do until 4 a.m. and not feel tired. It's what we love—what we were meant to do. That is your passion. And when you are working in your passion, you are channeling your "I Am" power directly from God. Few people are lucky enough to spend their lives earning a living from their passion, but that is usually because they do not try. We are taught to be "practical" when we should be inspirational! Let me share with you the Law of Passion:

~

YOUR PASSION CREATES THE FREEDOM TO ACHIEVE PROSPERITY.

~

You have to stay in the center of your passion. You must focus on what you love, no matter how your business grows. Hire people to do the tasks that your business needs to run and grow, but stay in your passion. Entrepreneurs often make the mistake of becoming successful and getting bogged down in the details of day-to-day operations, instead of spending their time doing what serves their passion—which is what made the business successful in the first place. Inventors should invent, cooks should cook, and musicians should make music. The passion is all.

How do you know if you are in the center of your passion? You will know, because you will feel the exaltation that comes from manifesting precisely what God intends you to manifest. God is love, and you were created with love. So figure out what you love and create a life around that. Do you love movies? Become a film critic. Do you love food? Become a chef and open a restaurant. Do you love cars? Start a business restoring and selling classic American cars. If you start with your passion, there are no wrong answers.

Passion Exterminates Work

Focusing on your passion also frees you. You don't need to grind at the details and management. When you have money, you don't need to force something to make money; you can be in the center of your passion and create something that reflects the Spirit within you. When you are working within your passion, you are free from work. Something that you are passionate about is never work; it's a pleasure. If you love it, you can do it for 16 hours a day and never get tired of it.

∼

WORK FROM YOUR PASSION AND YOU'LL NEVER WORK A DAY IN YOUR LIFE.

∼

It's great to be hungry, but be hungry in your spirit, not in your wallet. Money makes you free, and hunger and passion make you powerful. Listen to your passion and the Spirit inside you. Don't listen to the people who will tell you what you can't do. Don't be afraid. Your passion will generate profit. You must have a passion or you would not exist. If you don't know what your passion is, you must ask those four questions we talked about in the last chapter.

The Difference Between Passion and Purpose

I have spoken a great deal about purpose in this book. God has His purpose in you, and He wants you to have a purpose—or more than one purpose—for your life and the things you manifest in your life. Purpose gives life direction, meaning and momentum. However, purpose should not be the starting point for your life. That is the difference between passion and purpose.

If you are content to be a manager or technician, then purpose as a starting point is fine. Purpose without passion becomes little more than completing the steps on a to-do list; it will enable you to be productive and hold a job, but you will be a machine, completing tasks that you have set for yourself. As we have seen time and again, creativity is what produces wealth and profit. And passion produces creative energy.

Purpose without passion becomes little more than completing the steps on a to-do list

If your goal is to be an entrepreneur and use your creativity to manifest the things of Spirit that are now invisible, you must have passion as a starting point. Once you know your passion, your purpose will find you. Purpose without passion is empty; passion without purpose is impossible. Memorize this life equation to guide and inspire you:

PASSION + PURPOSE + ACTION = PROSPERITY

Once you have an inspiring, passionate vision and purposeful thought, you will feel the power of love working in you. You will begin to plan, adjust and act with boundless energy granted to you by God. You will be connected to an eternal power source that you cannot see, and you will begin to master your destiny.

Are You Caught in a Rut?

It's easy to fall into a rut of obligation instead of pursuing what you love. A job is a rut. Ask yourself, are you really obligated? If you are at a job only for the money, you're in a rut. But when you are in your passion, you know it: you're doing something where if the money was not there, you'd do it anyway.

No one has the power to permit you to do anything, to control what you can and cannot do. Even God cannot command what you can do. He can only make the choices available to you. You are truly free. You enter and stay in a rut by choosing to limit your choices.

Be what you want to be in your mind. You are not trying to do something; you *are* that thing! Misguided humility is lack of self-confidence in disguise. Be what you aspire to be! Take your purpose, begin to bring it into form with passion, purpose, thought, vision and word, and bring the Holy Spirit into it and fill that purpose with the Spirit and bring it into physical manifestation. It's time to let yourself out of prison!

Do not wait for someone to give you permission to be what you are. Declare what you are. The power of stating it is all. Don't wait for the money to show up; do and the money will follow. Courage, vision and Spirit attract money, people, passion and energy. Declare what you are and who you are and you make it manifest.

Be Yourself and Tap Your Divine Power

Are you inspired to take action, break out of your rut and find that Godlike passion that is burning within you? I hope so, because part of the purpose of this book is to awaken you to the truth: that you are an extraordinary being with the potential of becoming something greater: a co-creator with God. You have no reason to doubt your worth or your potential; God doesn't. You have only to accept the reality of your real self.

You probably did not know that your self is god. You are now discovering the god within you as you read this book. Your personality—the intellect and thoughts that you have thought were the real you—is meeting the Spirit that *is* the real you. You are a divine child and God is your father. You are god, and god is a higher version of you. And guess what? God is meeting you for the first time as well. You become real to Him when you become alive in Spirit. Meeting God is meeting yourself.

Your real self is a spiritual being. If you feel like you have not received the blessings that others have received, it is because you have not allowed you to be yourself. Others who have received blessings have received them because they developed the insight to set aside personality and open themselves to their true nature: divine beings who are guided by God. This has given them the key to tapping their own divine power. The real you in you brings forth freedom. Your mind is spirit invisible, and your body is Spirit materialized. You are Spirit having an earthly experience.

You Are an Act of Will

Wow, how huge is that? Well, let me blow your mind with something even more shocking:

∽

YOU ARE AN ACT OF WILL.

∽

You exist as a body of thoughts materialized. You bring yourself into real existence—Spirit existence—through the power of your mind. You are like the yogi: people took pictures of the yogi and other people, and while the other people showed up in the pictures, the yogi did not. Asked about the phenomenon, the yogi told the photographer it was because he, the yogi, was pure

Spirit. For the photographer to get his images, the yogi had to pose for him, to slow himself down, so he could be photographed.

You are exactly the same way, a being of Spirit inhabiting a physical presence. You may be self-conscious about your standing as a god, but once you understand it, you will become fully conscious of your power. Everything rises to meet you when you rise to your full level as a child of God. You will attract the people who are on your level when you rise to that level of consciousness. You must become who you are before you can attract the people who are like you. Then you will become the expression of what you desire!

The Cracked Plate

This is a lot to get your head around, but we're not done. When you are able to become in mind who you are in Spirit, things and people will begin to move toward manifestation in your life. However, they will not manifest at once. You will see signs. God works in harbingers: indicators of what is to come. This is for two reasons: to make sure that you retain your total trust in Him and your vision, and to allow you to prepare for the full manifestation. Often, the sign of the thing to come will be flawed or seem worthless, but one of the hallmarks that you are growing in vision and perception is that you can recognize that thing not as something worthless, but as a sign of what is about to come into your life.

It's like the woman who wished for a new set of dishes. A few days later, someone gave her a cracked plate. Instead of throwing it in the trash, she took it as a sign that her dishes were on their way. Sure enough, a few days later, someone donated to her a beautiful set of fine china that they did not need. That illustrates a basic principle:

~

THE APPEARANCE OF A "CRACKED PLATE" IN YOUR LIFE HERALDS THE COMING OF SOMETHING GREATER.

~

Think about it: seaweed lets sailors know land is near, but you can't stand on it. So you may have to spend time with people who are cracked plates because they are harbingers of the abundance that is to come later on. One dollar is a sign of a thousand to come. You put a little in a master's hand and it becomes plenty. Signs come; you will see when you are on the path. Stay on course and you will run into people who are on your same level. You will encounter people, things and events that indicate that you are on the right path. Look around and you will see the signs. One cracked plate will become a tea set, a place setting, and eventually a whole set of Mikasa china.

Look at new people who show up in your life; they are a sign of what's coming. Celebrate your cracked plate; it is a sign that good is to come.

* * *

SUMMARY

- You will never get rich at a job.
- God already knows your worth, but He can't pay you.
- The most important thing money buys is freedom.
- Passion creates prosperity.
- Only entrepreneurs create.
- You are a divine being waiting to come into your Self.
- You live by an act of your own will.
- A cracked plate is a sign of good to come.

Chapter 8

THE LAW OF THE VOW

———————

The power of the Word is unchallenged. God imagined Creation in His Mind, then brought it into manifestation with a Word. You have the ability to do the same—indeed, you have the *responsibility* to do it as part of your role as god. God is looking to you to help Him manifest His ideas and visions on this material plane. And though the Word can be expressed through thought and writing, the most powerful expression is through speech.

How is that possible, when we have spoken about the power of writing? The tongue is the mightiest tool of the Word because it is always available to you and you can reach others with it more easily than writing. Think about it: if someone is to read your Word, it first must be published in some way, as a book or on the Internet. But then you have no control over whether they will read your Word; you can't give someone a book and then hold a gun to their head and say, "Read!" But your spoken Word can reach them at any time, in any place. Your tongue can communicate your vision to one person or ten thousand at any time in any setting, and you control whether or not someone experiences your message.

The Tongue Can Set Nations on Fire

The tongue is small, but it can turn a life, a community or a nation around. Think of Jesus speaking to his disciples and what good that wrought for men. Think of Hitler speaking to the Germans and what evil that sparked. The tongue is the most potent weapon for good or ill that has ever been devised.

What you say will activate the Law of Attraction with greater intensity than any other mode of communication. You remember the Law of Attraction: what you speak or think will attract like things and people to you. Nothing does that more than ideas expressed in the spoken word. Great orators like Dr. King understood that perfectly; they know their words have the power to inspire and move nations. When you are in your power and have embraced the Spirit, your words will make you irresistible to those who are like you and can aid you.

People Must Remain in Your Life of Free Will

Thoughts of confidence, of passion, of vision, of courage will attract others. You will express the Spirit that will attract others. But real attraction is not just an ability to bring people into your life who serve your purpose, but to keep them there. When a person comes into your life through the Law of Attraction, they must stay of their own free will. God expects man and woman to keep their integrity of their being, not surrender it to someone else. When you try to possess someone else and hold them in place, you violate that integrity. This is a basic rule of the Laws of Thinking:

∼

IF A PERSON DOES NOT STAY IN YOUR LIFE OF THEIR FREE WILL, THEY DID NOT COME FROM GOD.

∼

Remember, God will only bring people into your life who will aid you. Anyone who does not stay is not inspired by your vision or motivated by the power of Spirit within you. And if they do not comprehend the "I Am" quality in you, they will not benefit your goals. Only when you allow freedom will you keep people in your life who you want there.

The Power of a Vow

There's an old saying that goes, "God loves to make a man break a vow." It's a reference the wrongheaded idea that pride is a sin, and it's not true. God loves a man who *keeps* a vow. Understanding what a vow is and what it means is one of the most important things you must do if you are to master the Laws and manifest all that God has in store.

A vow is an order of what you want to manifest in your life. It's a contract, a conditional bargain with God: "If You do this for me, I will do this for You." According to the dictionary, a vow is "an earnest promise to perform in a certain manner, especially a solemn promise to live and act in accordance with the rules of a religious order." It's a pledge that you will do what you say you will do.

THE LAWS OF THINKING

First of all, let's acknowledge that it is difficult to find any person who will keep a vow. Our society is carpeted with broken promises. It is very easy to make a vow, but apparently equally easy to violate it. Many people seem to misunderstand what a vow is:

~

YOUR VOW IS YOUR SPIRITUAL IDENTIFICATION CARD.

~

Think about it. When you strip away all of the identities that human society gives you—driver's license, passport, job title, resume, references from friends, even your name—what do you have left that tells others who you are? You have nothing except a question: Do you do what you say you will do? Do you keep your vows? *You are your vows.* There is no other currency in this world that you can spend with your fellow men.

Your Vow Opens the Floodgates

A vow is your key to the safe that holds God's intention to manifest good in your life. Jacob understood this, which is why he made a vow to God:

If God will be with me, and will keep me on this way that I go, and will give me bread to eat and raiment to put on, so that I come again to my father's house in peace, then shall the Lord be my God; and this stone, which I have set for a pillar, shall it be God's house; and of all that thou shalt give me I will surely give the tenth unto thee.
— Genesis 28:20-22

Jacob created a scenario so he could change his flock. He changed his future and fortune with a vow. When you are in a

94

hard place, that is your season to make a vow. That will make your place even harder, because it takes a harder stone to break the stone that imprisons you. A vow will often bring you to tougher times, because that is the only way you will be motivated to act to secure your freedom and allow God's intent to move in your life.

> *When you make a vow, God will start to speak. A vow is currency.*
>
> ~

But a vow also opens the sluice gates and immediately puts God to work beginning to manifest what you desire in your life. When you make a vow, God will start to speak. A vow is currency. It puts pressure on your covenant. You put a demand on your-self and therefore put a demand on God. That brings God in you forth. When you make a covenant, God silences your enemies. He handles your contract.

When you speak your vow, God does not wait for payment. He rolls up His sleeves and begins laboring in Spirit to create those things and people who serve your purpose and place them in that line of time that manifests them in your future physical experience— some in days, some in months, some in decades. But they are coming. That is the Law of the Vow:

~

WHEN YOU MAKE A VOW, GOD BEGINS ACTING
ON YOUR BEHALF IMMEDIATELY.

~

Keep your vow and be true and constant to your purpose and limitless wealth and opportunity will manifest in your life.

Break Your Vow, Suffer God's Wrath

Ah yes, the flip-side to the vow bargain you sign with the Almighty. Let's put it this way: how would you feel if you made a deal with someone where you would perform a very valuable service and he agreed to pay you handsomely for that service. You trust him, so you get to work. And after you have been working for weeks, he suddenly says, "I've decided I'm not going to pay you." You would be furious. You might take the guy to court to recover what he promised you, right?

That is exactly how God feels when you fail to keep your vow. When you make a vow to God, your part of the bargain is that you will:

A. Listen to what He says to you.

B. Act in Spirit without fear and doubt.

C. Declare your "I Am."

D. Keep a persistent focus on achieving your goals and manifesting what He has in mind for you.

When you fail to do those things, when you become distracted and drop your goals or when you let fear and doubt stop you, you betray your vow to God. If you do not keep your vow, failure will be yours and God will not care.

When a man is trying to please God, God makes even his enemies be at peace with him. If you stick to your vow, you can keep your enemies at bay no matter how hard they work to bring down what you are creating. But if you break your word, your vow will stand against you; it is proof that God cannot trust you to pay for services rendered. You will incur God's wrath and God's anger will destroy your works. You will lose protection from your enemies and

God will stop expressing his Spirit through you. You will be rudder-less, found unworthy to be an expression of the purpose of God.

Pay Your Vow as Soon as You Make It

Do not let your vow stand against you. Remember, you are your word. Your word is your only currency when everything else is stripped away. Will you be and do what you say you will do? If you keep your vow, blessings come. If you deny or betray it, you will receive a negative reward.

The world of men operates in the same way. A mortgage is also called a "first trust deed." The bank that loans you the money to buy your house is trusting that you will pay it back. If you break that trust, they will take away your house and put you in foreclosure. If you break your vow to God, He will foreclose on your dreams and visions. What happens when you go into fore-closure? Your credit gets ruined for years and it becomes much harder for you to get another lender to trust you in the future. The same thing happens with God. If you fail in your part of the covenant, God will be less likely to trust you with manifestation in the future.

When you make a vow, God expects that you will pay it in full. You don't get to eat the dinner, enjoy it, then say it was bad and not pay the bill. As the Bible says in Ecclesiastes 5: 4-5:

> *When thou vowest a vow unto God, defer not to pay it; for he hath no pleasure in fools: pay that which thou hast vowed. Better is it that thou shouldest not vow, than that thou shouldest vow and not pay.*

When you make a vow, there's an angel there. God watches over His Word, and will keep His Word. God always keeps His promises; He just does not tell you *how* He will keep His promise or *when* you will see the results. How He keeps His Word depends on how you keep your vow. You must avoid distraction and avoid things that will take you away from your vow.

Start paying the vow as soon as you make it. When you buy a house, you pay every month. Also, remember this:

~

DO NOT MAKE A VOW THAT IS TOO LARGE FOR YOU TO PAY BACK.

~

If you make the vow, God expects you to keep it. If it was too large a vow, that's your problem. Be aware of what you can handle. Your mortgage goes up when you buy a larger house, and if you can't make the payments, the bank takes your house away no matter what you say. You need to make a vow you can live in.

Are You Hanging Around the Cosmic Liquor Store?

God does not suffer procrastinators gladly. Procrastination is simply deferring or delaying paying your obligation to the Lord. God will destroy the works of your hands if you defer payment. Payment is consistent effort to fulfill the work of Spirit.

In the same way, God does not take kindly to loitering. Who is it that loiters around the entrance to stores and businesses? Vagrants, bums, drunks and people with absolutely nothing to do . . . no choices to make. Loiterers are failures, because they have nothing better to do with their time than waste it. They do not contribute. If you are loitering in life and wasting time instead of working in God's Word, you will get picked up. You're standing around without purpose, so you're vulnerable to any doctrine or distraction to blow you away from your vow.

There are loiterers in my church, Zoe Ministries, and in every church. They could be people who have been saved in Christ, but who understand nothing about God's system. These people hang around as vagrants, without a purpose, without tithing, without vows, without any commitment other than showing up on Sunday morning. And in return, they're hoping to get something for nothing from God. They are taking up space and blocking the path for everyone else. They are opting for the deferment plan.

In a busy life, there's no loitering. You have purpose and you are making things happen!

Let me tell you something you'd do well to remember:

GOD DOES NOT REWARD YOU
FOR JUST SHOWING UP!

In a busy life, there's no loitering. You have purpose and you are making things happen! If you want something done, ask a busy person. Busy people are rarely still; they are making choices, creating opportunity, and wielding the Law of Attraction. Busy = Purposeful = Rich.

The poor loiterer has no plans for their time. The poor drop in, because when you don't have purpose, you won't make appointments. When you're rich your time is valuable and there's always more to do, so you make appointments and keep a schedule. Why? You have a purpose to serve.

Loiterers never contribute. God doesn't get excited about amounts given; He cares about what's left over. How much of yourself do you give? Do you give of yourself consistently and give enough so that you are depending on God to be your supply, not paycheck? Do you empty your bank account knowing that God will fill it higher than before? Money wants to be moved around. It's like anything else in life: it's evolving and never static. God makes things happen when you move money around.

How Are You Breaking Your Vow?

Sin is as simple as breaking your vow and forfeiting the good that was coming your way. Your sin does not hurt God, except for His feelings; all the harm you do is to yourself. Remember, an angel is present when you make your vow; if you break your vow, you anger your angel, and that is something I do not advise!

If you are not manifesting in your life that which you desire, then you are breaking a vow to God in some way. How could you be breaking your vow? You should be asking yourself this critical question. God was ready to kill Moses because he had not kept a vow to circumcise his sons. His wife circumcised them instead and told Moses, "You serve a bloody god." When failure is coming into your life, look around and look back and figure out how you could be betraying your covenant with God. There are many possible ways:

- Allowing yourself to become distracted.

- Allowing fear or doubt to stop you from acting.

- Playing it too safe.

- Letting yourself be ruled by money.

- Giving someone else control over you.

Your vow will always be tested. Contrary things and people will always appear. Controversy will arise immediately to see if you will persevere in your vow. Remember that God will always test you to make you stronger. What must you do to become an "overcomer?"

* * *

SUMMARY

- The most powerful Word is the spoken word.

- People must remain in your life of their own free will.

- Your promise is your only currency.

- A vow starts God working for you immediately.

- God expects you to keep your part of your vow.

- God will punish you for loitering or procrastinating.

- Your vow will always be tested.

Chapter 9

THE LAW OF THE WORD

———————

We're moving now away from the broader Laws of Thinking and into the more precise principles that dictate how God works within the system that He created. One of those principles involves the role that prophecy plays in your awareness of God's message to you and how you are asked to do your part to make it manifest. But before we look at how to get, let's look at the idea of giving things up.

Sometimes, God shuts down income you're making because He's trying to show you new income. God does not act with malice, but when He perceives that you are worshipping a false idol, He will step in and shock you into remembering by removing that idol from your life. If you get too comfortable with something, God shuts it down. When you are too comfortable with something, it has become the center of your life; you perceive it as the source of the good in your life. There is only one source of good, and that's God. So by stripping away what you had come to rely on, God reminds you that He must be at the center of your world.

103

That's not ego. God has an ego, because if He did not, we would not. But He doesn't take things away from you because He feels slighted; He does it because if you are depending on money, fame, technology or anything else to be the center of your success, your success will be built on the flesh and therefore it will not last. It will become corrupt. All things based on the flesh do. It's only when you continue to hold God at the center and make His Spirit the source of your power and prosperity that what you create will be truly lasting. God's doing you a favor, though He can seem like a tough taskmaster.

You Must Give Things Up

You have probably heard the phrase, "You only get what you give." There is no piece of wisdom that more perfectly encapsulates the Laws of Thinking. The Universe is an economy, and you do not receive anything unless you give something first. When you walk into a store and want to buy groceries, you have to hand over money before you can walk out the door. When you give, a mystical transfer of "ownership" takes place and suddenly, you possess something you did not just a few seconds before. That's a bargain we make in society, and we have all made the same bargain with the Almighty. You get, you must give.

You must give things up for God to bring more to you.

You must give things up for God to bring more to you. When you release something, God brings you more. This means that you must be willing to surrender things of value to you without thought of what you will receive in return. It could be money given to your church or to a charity. It could be ending your involvement with an important customer of your business because they do not operate ethically, even though they provide 50% of your income. It could be severing ties with a partner who is holding you back. God only cares that you give up something of value, because that shows that God remains the source of good things for you.

When you let things go—when you get excited about giving— God will open doors for you and make things happen. Get excited, because God is excited about giving to you. When you give as a part of your personal culture, you call God on His part of the agreement. You say, "God, I'm casting away a large part of what You have helped me build so far, because I trust that You will bring me more." When you do that, God must respond, because that is part of the covenant He has created with you. You will find that the money you give comes back to you tenfold, one lost customer turns into five better ones, and your former partner becomes the path to a host of new people who will empower and inspire you.

People Need People

Speaking of people, let's talk about them for a moment. If Spirit and your vow are the currency of the cosmic economy, then people are the engine that runs it. Remember that you are a vessel for Spirit to manifest its intentions on this plane. Without people, there would be no way for God to bring forth His plans and ideas in this world. No one succeeds alone, no matter what he or she thinks. Even the most solitary of writers, composers or artists needs other people to bring their inspired works to the world— editors, musicians, gallery owners.

You will only reach the heights God has in mind with other people. You need a network of people who will inspire, encourage and challenge you. We all need people to connect us to various

aspects of God. Jesus would not have been born without a con-
nector, a network of people. That was why John the Baptist was
born to Elizabeth. He was Jesus' anchor in this world.
Connections are everything. Every person you get to know will be
a gateway to something good or something bad. It's your job to
recognize what each person is a gateway to and walk through the
gateways that lead to what you want.

You cannot get where you are going without other people.
Whatever God gives you will come to you through other people.
It will not drop out of the sky. However, other people are also your
potential curse, which is why honing your perceptions and
remaining honest with yourself are so vital. Self-delusion is perhaps the purest form of sin. You must be honest with yourself
about the people in your life. Because whenever the devil wants
to take something from you, he will raise up a man to take it from
you. Connections are both our strength and our weakness. You
must watch who walks with you.

Mission Impossible?

Among the people you do want to have in your life are
prophets. I said earlier in the book that all of us are our own self-
fulfilling prophets, but legitimate prophets are those individuals
who will help you discern what God's decrees and the events of
your life mean in relation to God's plan for you.

Prophets do not have any more ability than you to hear God's
Word; we all possess the ability to hear God. Where the prophets
are different is that they know how to listen: in Spirit, not in
sound. Remember, God is pure Spirit and Spirit can only speak to
Spirit. You can have ability to hear, but if you do not know how to
listen, you will remain ignorant of God's intentions for you.

Prophets listen to God in Spirit and analyze the things and people that come into your life so that you can perceive the hidden patterns in what God is doing.

Without the help of prophecy, the loss of a job might appear to you to be nothing more than a tragedy that drives you to the edge of bankruptcy. But with the guidance of a prophet who understands how God's system works, you can begin to see how losing your job, plus other events and people that have come into your life at the same time, are actually signs of a greater blessing to come—a call to action for you from the Lord. So it is with most of the twists and turns of our lives—they can become blessings and opened doors if you have the right guidance to help you see them for what they really are.

The reason the prophets are so important to you is that God will often give you a prophecy that looks like an impossibility. He will communicate to you that you are to become a multi-millionaire and the founder of an entire new industry, such as He did to the people who created rap and hip-hop. And because any manifestation always begins as an invisible thought before it starts to become real in your experience, if you're not enlightened by a prophet, you'll say to God, "Impossible. I can't do that." Even if you are steeped in Spirit and ready to go forth and risk it all for God, you might still feel like it's too great a leap for you to make. Prophets clue you in to the signs that accompany prophecy, signs that tell you what you should be doing and who you should be meeting.

That is why it is so crucial to understand when God is speaking a Word to you. You must know it and listen, because you will be unable to act to manifest that Word if you think it's an impossibility.

Prophecy Is Everywhere

Great changes are always foretold by the appearance of prophetic events. Prophetic events are like the vanguard of disruptive change to come, like the vanguard of a huge army that comes a few days later. God will always speak a prophetic Word, because your own word can harm the manifestation of what is coming. Remember how God made Zacharias dumb until his son, John the Baptist, was born? That's because a word of doubt from Zacharias that such a birth was "impossible" could have aborted the divine pregnancy in his wife's belly. God lets you know big things are on the way so you'll keep quiet, avoid doubtful words and thoughts, and let Him go on manifesting.

> *God will always speak a prophetic Word, because your own word can harm the manifestation of what is coming.*

Jesus' birth was filled with prophecy. The angel Gabriel came to Mary and told her she would bear a child, even though she had "known not a man." The attack by Herod on the infants was a sign: an attack on children is always a signal that deliverers and light bringers are being born in the earth.

Why were the three wise men called wise? Because they understood that prophecy was in the air. They did not return to their homes the same way they came; if they had, they would have likely been killed by the soldiers of the fearful king. A wise man never goes back the same way he came. A man can come into a church homeless, but leave later with many homes. You never come into contact with the power of prophecy and come away unchanged . . . if you are in a state of mind and Spirit to listen and recognize the prophecy.

The Heroic Cycle

This business of listening to God and recognizing His Word is complex, isn't it? That's why there were few true prophets in the Bible, such as Isaiah, but it's also why the false prophet has been scorned throughout history as a bringer of evil. Can you imagine a person who, either through malice or self-deception, interpreted a prophecy in a way that took you farther away from God's purpose? How might that ruin your life? You must always exercise care in which prophets you listen to.

One way to do that is to understand the basic rules of God's system. One of these is this:

~

GOD ALWAYS HIDES YOUR TREASURE IN AN UNLIKELY VESSEL.

~

God never shows up in something that looks the way you think it should look. He always buries the treasure in a vessel that looks unlike it would hold the treasure. In the case of Jesus, he sent the deliverer of Man in the person of a humble, poor carpenter who taught about love and kindness. Wouldn't it have been more appropriate—certainly more Hollywood—to send a Messiah who was a charismatic warrior? That's not how God works. He never places anything into your hand. He offers and you must choose. That is how you learn wisdom.

God will always send deliverance that looks nothing like deliverance, so that you will be forced to walk a path to discover and reap that deliverance. God wants the process of you manifesting His will to change you, to transform you into a divine being. That is why every generation has its tales of unlikely heroes taking a journey to move from ignorance and obscurity to knowledge, struggle, self-awareness and finally victory, from Cinderella to Star Wars. That's the heroic cycle made famous by the late writer Joseph Campbell: the hero has a revelation, leaves his home, makes a journey fraught with peril, discovers his own flaws and strengths, and is changed by the experience.

God Uses Rejects

To pursue that thought even further, you could say that God is likely to take what others perceive as the most unworthy of a society and elevate them to the highest places in His purpose. In reality, every one of us has the potential to be "I Am" and take our place as God's junior partner, but the more humble a person is, the more likely he or she is to be willing to set aside ego and intellect to open the mind and listen completely to what God is saying.

To put it another way, who do you think is more likely to listen when God speaks: a successful surgeon with a BMW and a fancy mansion, or a failed inventor who has been told by everyone that his ideas stink? The greater your rejection, the greater your anointing. God uses rejects. If you have not been rejected, you are not worthy to be used.

How is that possible? There is logic behind the idea. If you are not being rejected, you are not riding the edge and stepping outside your comfort zone and stretching to do great things. All original thinkers—artists, scientists, inventors, entrepreneurs—are told they are insane or heretics before they try their ideas. Only after the ideas manifest are they called geniuses. But to be such a genius—to be exalted in the eyes of God—you must first risk everything and *embrace* being rejected. Stop looking to be accepted and look for rejection.

The death of Jesus was about being rejected. The destroying of self must precede rejection. You will not be lifted up by God and come into your "I Am" inheritance until you can lie down and get rejected until the Spirit raises you up. If you are comfortable, you have placed money or things at the source of your power, and only God can be that source. That is why rejects are more likely to hear God and respond. They have let go of self and are open to the message. They accept God's special delivery!

Don't Strip Your Future to Pay for the Present

Prophecy is not designed to scare you. It is designed to make you aware. Never be afraid of the future, because the future is not afraid of you. We start to come now to the economics of God's manifestation, the material I covered in my book *Cosmic Economics*. In the economy of the Universe, you are the currency and you spend that currency with your mind operating in Spirit.

In the cosmic economy, your future is only as rich as your present, and you will always have to pay for tomorrow that which you take from your present today. Giving to others is stripping your present to enhance your future. It is sowing to reap later, and the act will always bring you good fortune. That is why people who tithe generously to their church without thought of what they are going to get seem to have good fortune coming their way all the time. They know that giving is paying for the invisible to come.

Borrowing, on the other hand, is stripping your future to enhance your present. Instead of letting go and giving, you take from what you have in account father along your timeline and use it to add to what you have now. You have put something else before God as your source. You are emptying your seeds, and when you empty the seeds, you will reap a poor harvest.

The more you sow—the more you lay down and let go of what is not God and trust God to lift you up into your purpose, the more that will come to you. You might have no home, then own several homes, or have no car, then own several cars. The potential is without limit . . . once you know the system.

Your Prophetic Word

Let's get right to the Law of the Word:

⁓

YOUR WORDS HAVE THE POWER TO CREATE OR ABORT.

⁓

How does this relate to what has gone before in this chapter? It all goes back to understanding. Just as you must listen to the prophet in order to comprehend the meaning of God's speech, you must understand the power of your own words to either serve or defy prophecy.

If you don't believe a prophecy, your words will kill it. Worse, they will send it to someone else. Your words and thoughts can produce life or death. That's why you have to watch flattery. Watch low self-esteem. Words can grow in you and steer your mind. Be careful about listening to people who are not going in your direction. Words contain something that is coming back to you.

As has probably become clear to you though the reading of this book, the vast majority of human beings are asleep to God's Word, their own divinity and their own potential. We sleep collectively, but we arise individually at a time when and if we are ready to set aside the self and become a vessel for God to pour His thoughts into. Some individuals wake up when they hear the right Word; some people should not be awakened at all, because they will never hear. For them, ignorance is bliss. Others are turning over in their sleep, but that doesn't mean they're waking up. Know this:

~

WHEN YOU HEAR GOD'S WORD, RECOGNIZE IT FOR WHAT IT IS, AND IF YOU ARE READY TO ACT ON IT, YOU ARE AWAKE.

~

Your Thoughts Are Angels

Every one of your thoughts is an angel speaking to you. Gabriel convinced Mary that even though she had not known a man, she would become pregnant and carry the child who would become Jesus. The lesson is not lost on you: you, too, can give birth to a miracle without knowing a man. You can create without any visible means of support, without the means that you think you must have to achieve the goal. All you need to do is take the thing in your hands and do. Believe the Word of your angel and the means to achieve what you set out to do will appear.

Know that, like Mary and many others, you must go through the dark night of the soul, where it's just you and God and there is nothing to buoy your spirits except your faith that God will provide if you step out into thin air and risk falling. There is something you are pregnant with, something you must give birth to. Speak a word and make it so.

* * *

SUMMARY

- You must give things up to receive more.

- You need people to achieve your goals.

- God will always give you a prophecy that appears impossible.

- Wrenching events are a sign that prophecy is taking place.

- God sends deliverance in unlikely vessels.

- God chooses rejects for His purposes.

- Your word can birth or kill your ideas.

Chapter 10

THE LAW OF MIND

———————

It is common in the system of the Lord that what is a great asset is at the same time a potential threat. It's the classic double-edged sword concept: one edge can defend and win battles; the other can turn on you and wound or maim you. It's all in knowing how to wield the weapon. That is the nature of the mind, the intellect, and the emotions in hearing and channeling the Word of God.

In opening yourself to the flood of insight and revelation from God, intellect can be your worst enemy. Knowing too much can blind you to the new and unknown. Intellect is the portion of your mind that contains your ego, the part of your personality that thinks it knows the nature of reality and how the Universe works. Your intellect is God to itself. And this barrier can stand in the way of the flow of Spirit from the incorporeal realm that begins manifesting good in your life.

You must be able to set aside intellect—to stop trying to analyze and simply feel what is happening. There is incredible power in allowing yourself to feel the reality of God's vision, feel it become as real and tangible as if it were already achieved in materiality. This is the key to manifestation: envision how you would feel if you were in a Rolls Royce. Give yourself the expression and feeling of having the Rolls and the Rolls will have no choice but to come into your experience.

> *Feeling and the body are connected. Put on the feeling and the body will come.*
>
> ∿

Feeling and the body are connected. Put on the feeling and the body will come. You can't get good until you feel good. Capture the feeling and the body of that experience is near. Embracing the feeling is a way of transcending the limits of your intellect and trusting your Spirit to tell you what is real.

The Importance of Meditation

By meditation, you can be what you envision. Meditation (if you are uncomfortable with the word because it suggests Eastern religions or mysticism, you can use *prayer*) is the process by which you put your mind in a state where you are open to receiving God's Word in Spirit. When you meditate, you become a two-way radio with the receiver turned up as high as it will go. And when you can let go of intellect and stop trying to analyze the experience—when you can stop being and start becoming one with God—then you will feel some amazing insights and visions enter your mind.

I meditate daily. So does every prophet. We all have our own rituals around our meditation, but we all do it because that is the only way we can quiet our minds, still our thoughts and really *listen* to God. The ego and the intellect are heavy; it takes some serious lifting even for the most experienced, anointed prophet to clear them out of the path of God's signal.

Meditation helps you feel . . . *really* feel. As Jesus made the men sit down in the biblical account of the loaves and fishes, meditation makes the mind sit down, quells the part that only sees facts, sees doubt. You sit the mind down, count backward from five to one, and you get into a state of being like a child, where you are trusting and unquestioning. This feeling will woo manifestations into your life.

Becoming "as a little child" is an act of going to a deeper level of mind, becoming simpler, entering an alpha state of consciousness where you can hear the Word of God. Meditation opens up the imagination, which is where all the things you hope to manifest will exist before they ever exist in the physical. There's even significance in the fact that many advanced meditation practitioners tilt their eyes at a 45-degree angle when they enter this state of consciousness. This forces you to look upward as a child does to her Father. Meditation at this level goes beyond the mind to where your pure creative energy holds sway.

God Only Responds to "I Am"

There's a very good reason to master the skill of letting go of intellect and quieting your mind: it is the only way God will pay attention to your desires and manifest what you want in your life. God does not listen to reasoning or intellect, because they only deal in the actual, what already exists. But we have already seen that when what you want first begins to manifest, it will be invisible and appear impossible. Asking with your intellect automatically says to God, "I want this thing in my life." It's a statement of want, an admission that you and your desire are separate. You are not separate:

117

~

YOU AND YOUR DESIRE MUST BE ONE FOR IT TO MANIFEST.

~

God will never give you a want. He only answers "I Am," because He only answers to His name. He is always listening for it. God is listening for you to declare your true nature as "I Am," to become the things that you want, before He can begin manifesting them for you. You must be the house, the car, the contract. As long as you are separate from them, you are in want, and want robs you of your power! Whatever you add "I Am" to, God brings it into your life. Temptation is in longing and wanting; Spirit is always "I Am," and no there is no temptation.

You must learn to listen for your nature. Once you can live something in your imagination, you are in receiving mode and you will bring the thing into manifestation. Once you are conscious of being, you will become.

The Mind Has to Be Taught to Die

It's ironic that the mind, God's greatest creation, is also the thing that hinders us the most from receiving His favor. But that's how God works: everything is a potential struggle or barrier that you must gain wisdom to surmount. That is never more true that with the mind. You have to teach your mind to exist in the form of imagination while lying dormant in the area of intellect. You have to teach your mind to die. If you don't, your word or doubt can kill what God is trying to manifest for you.

I heard a story a few years ago of a man who got sick and had six months to live. During the period after his diagnosis, he fell in love with growing orchids. Orchids consumed him, became his passion. A year later, he was asked how he was still alive after the doctors all predicted he wouldn't make it more than six months. "I forgot to die," he said. He lived for years after that.

Your mind, the rational part of you that thinks it knows more than God, has to be taught to shut up, lie down, go into a coma for a while. Following the Word of God is a feeling in your belly, a sense of synchronicity, an impulse to act that has no basis in logic but just feels right. When you follow such feelings as your prime movers, you are acting in accordance with Spirit and on your way to becoming the things you want. Even the most brilliant scientific minds of all time, masters of rational thinking, admitted that many of their greatest breakthroughs occurred when their minds took intuitive leaps. That was surely what happened when God gave Albert Einstein a stunning insight into the structure underlying the cosmos with the Theory of Relativity, which changed our understanding of how the Universe works.

Freeing the mind from the intellect opens you up to capture a constant stream of inspiration and intuition that is always flowing past and around you.

Names Define Your World

This leads us to the concept of naming, and the fact that when you name something or someone, you define their nature. Names carry vibration, and vibration carries nature. The meaning of your name and the names of others will tell you where you are in the process of achieving the state of being that allows you to see the Word coming to you.

How you name things reveals much about how you regard the world. If you are aware of the power of naming, then you will exercise care in what you name the things and people in your life—and how you name yourself. For the name of a thing not only reveals its true nature, it sets the definition of its nature in motion. In naming something or someone, you alter its nature.

Naming draws on energy, either positive or negative. Naming yourself, for example, a negative name pushes your Spirit into the negative and begins to attract negative results and people to you. The opposite is true if you give yourself positive names. Like so much else in the Laws of Thinking, you must be (and name) yourself what you want to become in order to bring that thing to you in material manifestation. Name yourself what you want to become—a millionaire, a CEO—in order to become that thing. Name the people you will have in your life—investors, partners—before they arrive and you call them into being.

Faith Shall Be Rewarded

All this material comes back to one central idea: setting aside what you think you "know" with your intellect and having *faith* in God. God rewards faith. Faith is the most important thing He asks of you. It is not because God wants flattery; He doesn't need empty words. God asks for faith because that is the way He can work through each of us. Faith opens the door to favor.

Faith requires that you suspend the usual expectations that good will come immediately. We are an instant gratification culture, but God does not operate on our timeline. There are seasons that God will allow you to walk so that He appears He is not with you, so He can come back and spin you out of adversity. That is the way

God works: provoking you, challenging you, surprising you into exceeding what you thought were your limitations.

Sometimes, all you need to do is ask for grace and God brings things into your life. Grace is unmerited favor from God—favor you do not deserve but He gives anyway. We spoke about favor and the concept of the Favor-ite. Remember, favor is not fair! But when you have faith and you ask for favor, favor will get you what faith cannot. God's favor will give you something when your faith doesn't have time to manifest it. Think of faith as the slow postal carrier of your vision, and favor as UPS Next Day. Sometimes, you need the thing immediately, and favor manifests it.

> *God's favor will give you something when your faith doesn't have time to manifest it.*

The favor that faith produces will confound and anger others who think you are thumbing your nose at their authority, and more important, at the way they think the world is supposed to work. Favor will make the prosecutor mad. Situations will not work against you even though they should. You will walk out of situations that should condemn you. God will be smiling upon you. Favor rewards faith, not logic or intellect. If your purpose in life is to please God, good things will come into your life.

Baptism Drowns Your Higher Mind

Here's the trouble with all this: we take pride in being rational creatures. Human beings are enamored of our reason, and we should be: it's an incredible tool that has enabled us to create wonderful things. But it has its limitations, chief of which is that reason can only function in the world of the material. It is useless in the Spirit realm. That is why feeling and faith rule there. But training your mind to let go of reason and be ruled by intuition is very difficult. That is why you must baptize your mind, drown your intellect and be reborn as a Spiritual mind.

How do you do this? Through the consistent, persistent practice of meditation and the letting go of ego. Intellect will compel you to rely on mind and deny Spirit, and you have to fight a constant battle to keep your denial down and listen to Spirit. Your mind must be a conduit for God's mind. Baptism buries doubt and intellectual thoughts. Your higher mind is washed away and there is room for God's voice and mind to take up residence in you.

That's why John was the Baptist: baptism is done on the head, because your thoughts must be baptized, pushed down. You must drive away thoughts that get in the way of Spirit. Now, let me say something important. None of this means that you should reject the work of your intellect in other circumstances. Christianity is far too full of people who have an anti-intellectual bent; they fear people who ask too many questions about matters of faith, because they are using their faith as a pillar to hold up some kind of earthly temple that has nothing to do with God, such as money or hatred.

True believers know that God created the intellect to make us curious and to help us innovate and invent and advance humankind. God is also Intellect as well as Spirit. The problem comes when intellect does not know its proper place: as a tool of the material, not the Spiritual. You must relegate your rational mind to its place and bring out your faith and your inspiration when you deal with matters of the Spirit. Intellect is nothing to fear; it simply does not work with God's system. It works with Man's.

Never Ask God How

So, you are operating in faith and opening your feelings to God and declaring yourself "I Am" the things you desire. That's wonderful. Just avoid doing one bad thing: never ask God *how* He is going to manifest things in your life. It's none of your business, and God doesn't want your advice on how He should make things happen.

Tell God what you want and leave it. Don't instruct Him how, don't tell Him who to bring it, and don't instruct as far as time and place. Ask and be quiet. Then when the thing is delivered, don't judge it. Just accept it. Let it be and let it manifest. When you begin to ask how and where and when, you're installing your intellect over the mind of God, and that doesn't work. God will send signs (the cracked plate) to you to let you know when something is beginning to manifest, but that's probably all He will do. Why? Because He wants you to develop the insight to see the beginnings of manifestation for yourself . . . to hone your perceptions and gain a greater comprehension of prophecy.

The Law of Mind

All things must have a *psychogenesis*, a beginning in the realm of mind. The physical manifestation is merely the lingering after-effect of that which has already taken place in the invisible world of mind. What occurs in the mind is a transaction between you and God, an exchange of your attention for His Word that brings Spirit into manifestation. You pay and you receive. You could say that the physical manifestation that follows is nothing more than a reflection of the true manifestation that occurs in your mind and the invisible world of Spirit.

The Law of Mind:

~

MIND IS THE INVISIBLE WORLD OF IMAGINATION WHERE ALL THINGS ARE FIRST CREATED.

~

You must mentalize it before you can materialize it!

~

Do not confuse mind and intellect; intellect is the rational, doubting pragmatist we've bashed so much in this chapter. Mind is the part of your personality that soars beyond limits and imagines the impossible, thereby making it possible. When you see something in your imagination, it eventually comes into the body of your experience, assuming you remain focused and persistent in your desire for it. What moves in the invisible realm of mind gets things moving in the visible world of the material. You must *mentalize* it before you can *materialize* it!

As you strive to master all this information, remember the definition of faith: faith is the substance of things hoped for and the evidence of things unseen. Everything you need already exists in the mind of God, which has no time. Everything you are to be and become already exists. You have only to call it up and make it manifest in your imagination. Listen to God telling you where to find it, and bring it forth with your attention and thought.

Be Aware and Let Manifestation Happen

My, this is a lot to work on! The skills of listening to God, turning your being over to feeling and imagination, may run counter to everything you think you know about being human. We're taught to respect only reason; that it is what separates us from the lower animals. But that is not true. What sets man apart is his divine nature as "I Am," his power to become a creator, to shape the unseen world and therefore the material world as well. So as you learn to work in the world of Spirit, cultivate your awareness of things and people changing around you.

Signs will become visible as things start to manifest for you. People will come into and out of your life. God will speak to you. You must always be aware of what is happening around you and understand what it means. If you are not aware, you may miss a sign or an opportunity and end up damaging your manifestation.

Do your work, then rest your mind and let your desire take shape as experience. It cannot take shape as long as you are still working on it in the realm of your mind. You need to come to a conclusion in your mind. Psychogenesis cannot take place until you rest your mind. Take your hands off the wheel, let God drive, and allow things to manifest in whatever shape they see fit. You cannot control the shape or nature of the manifestation; simply recognize it and find a way to work with it.

* * *

SUMMARY

- Your intellect gets in the way of God's communication.

- Meditation is the critical discipline to master in hearing God's Word.

- God does not respond to want, only to "I Am."

- The mind has to be trained to lie down and be still.

- When you name a thing, you define its nature.

- Baptism is a drowning of the doubting higher mind.

- Never ask God how He plans to manifest.

- All creation starts in the imagination.

Chapter 11

THE LAW OF THE JOURNEY

———•———

There are mysteries within mysteries within the Laws of Thinking and the system by which God operates. This is the study of years, which is why the prophets are so important. It takes a prophet to begin to make sense of all that is assaulting you from every side. That's why as you learn, it is so vital for you to begin doing the basics you need to do to put God's expression to work on your behalf: speak Words of creation and life, and prophesy until something happens. You come into this world pregnant with the Word and the possibility of creation, but you must push something out into the visible realm. It's not easy (as any woman who has gone through childbirth can tell you) but you can't get it any other way.

You must take notice of where you are. You must enhance your faculties of perception and know who you are and what you want to be. If you don't know what you want, you won't have it. The process we are all called to follow requires us to exercise control and then give it up: to begin manifesting, we must control our minds and come to a conclusion: "I Am this thing, this goal, this desire." Then once we know that, we must cede control to God and say, "I trust you, Lord, and I will act without concern for money or risk and let You work your will." All the while, we must control our words and thoughts so we do not torpedo our boat before it's launched. That is a difficult balancing act, and learning the skill to master it takes decades. That is why you rarely see successful people in their 20s; they're still making their mistakes and tripping over their own words.

Give Up Your Mind

In the end, you must be willing to give up your mind—the intellect part of you that tries to direct the show—so a greater mind can take over. John the Baptist symbolizes this; he had to be beheaded to be resurrected with the mind of Christ. The key to Man is his thoughts. You are your thoughts. The mind of Man is the mouth of God. God created you as a conduit for His Word on this plane.

If you recall, we said earlier that God has no presence on this plane without you. He can only manifest Creation—Creation can only reach its fruition—with you acting under the guidance of God. God does not want to pull your strings like a puppet, but to channel His Word through you and let you shape the ends. With that kind of energy working through your mind and Spirit, you cannot help but do great things. But first, you have to get ego and self-importance out of the way!

Your Diamonds Are Waiting to Be Dug Up

For he shall be great in the sight of the Lord, and shall drink neither wine nor strong drink; and he shall be filled with the Holy Ghost, even from his mother's womb.
— Luke 1:15

Everything that Man needs, everything you need to fulfill your destiny, already exists in the Universal Mind that is God. It is as if the prosperity and greatness you wish for yourself is buried in the earth as diamonds. No man created the diamonds that end up on an engagement ring; they were created by natural processes that God set in motion and endowed with Spirit, and they lay hidden until some miner dug them up.

> *What you want to become is sleeping in you. You must transform your mind to awaken it.*
>
> ～

In exactly the same way, everything you desire is waiting, hidden, already fully formed, waiting for you to discover it, dig it up, and polish it to perfection. Everyone is fulfilling a path in earth, a path ordained by God. You are already fully formed as who you will be in your own "I Am" consciousness; you just have to surrender your doubtful intellect, say "I Am that experience," and use the power of the Word to bring those things to yourself. What you want to become is sleeping in you. You must transform your mind to awaken it.

Talents that you possess, ideas you will one day bring to fruition—they all lie dormant in your Spirit right now, at this very moment! That's exciting—the potential to change your own life is within you even as you read this book. But you must act and transform your thought processes in order to take that potential energy and turn it into kinetic energy that creates change. I'll bet you didn't realize that the forces you need to bring yourself closer to the life you have imagined were so close at hand. Most people do not. They are busy looking outward for those forces, when they should be looking inward at the diamonds that God placed in them at the Creation.

The spiritual man, or Christ, the Word of God, is the true inner self of every individual. Man, therefore, contains within himself the capacities of Becoming, and through his Words, uses the creative principles of Divine Mind to create.

Patience, Grasshopper

Once you do reach that level of mental awareness where you can become the Word and open the gates for God to create in Spirit, you may think that's the end of the process. All you have to do now it sit back and catch all the good things as they arrive, right? Wrong. God never makes it that easy. He vows to bring you manifestation, but he does not say *when*.

Usually, manifestation comes long after the decision is made. During the long gestation period, the thing you want is going to ask you every day, "Are you sure you want me?" That's why patience and persistence of effort and focus are so important. The blessing will come in its own good time. Once you declare your "I Am" and open to the Word, God will bring it to you. But the timing is not in your control.

God will test your faith and focus even while He is slowly assembling what you want in the spiritual realm. All the new surprises that come along while you're waiting for what you want to manifest are tests of your faith. A little bit of doubt can drive what you are becoming from your mind, and therefore, from your life. You will always be tested, because God only shows favor to those who endure.

This is why it is essential to have the capacity of *being*. Rather than worrying about what you can do, focus on who you are. *You are the thing you want!* How strongly you declare that you *are* that experience will pull the people you need to make happen what you want to make happen. Your "I Am" creates the allies you need to manifest what you want. Be; don't worry about what you can do.

The Sin of the Prodigal Son

When you begin to tap the power of your own Divine Mind, you connect yourself to God's economy, the cosmic system of payment and receipt that governs all things. This is where all children must be, interwoven with their father's economy and earning what enables them to create change. When you achieve wealth, but let that wealth become the most important thing to you, you are in sin. The sin of the prodigal son was becoming separate from his father's economy. God doesn't care that you're wealthy, but that your wealth does not become the source of all things for you. God must always be the source of what you need. If you are looking outside yourself for your dreams, you will never find them. They are inside you. They *are* you.

But even if you do separate yourself from God in this way, He will not correct you. God likes hard lessons, because He knows that we, His willful children, seldom learn from any other kind of experiences. God is not interested in becoming the savior of His children. You should never become the savior for *your* children. You are their teacher, but they must act of their own will and their own mind. God did not save creation, but sent His Son and let His Son save creation of his will.

When the prodigal son wanted to play the fool, his father allowed him. The father allowed him to have the experience, because it was the only way he would learn. You will only be saved when you come to yourself and realize that God knows more than you do. That is why the tough lessons and hard knocks of life exist: to teach you.

131

Stay Hungry

All this material is leading us to a logical conclusion:

~

YOU WON'T BE FILLED BY GOD
UNTIL YOU ARE HUNGRY.

~

Most of us have to reject God and experience the want that rejection creates before we understand the hunger that makes us crave being with God. You will think you have all the answers; we all do. You will be lost in some way. You may hit bottom and be in despair. Only then will you make the decision to seek out God, to seek answers and discover the aspect of God within you.

As a parent, you must turn your child loose to reach a place of waste. Only when you are perishing with hunger will you be as a child, seeking the wisdom of the Universal Mind. That remains the hardest decision any parent must face: to let his or her child suffer and fail, knowing that while a word of wisdom might set the child on the right track, wisdom that does not come from within is as temporary as rain puddles in the sunshine. Truly loving parents endure and let their children struggle and scrape to find their way, because they know that is the only way one gains true wisdom and the desire to turn inward. God does the same with all of us.

That's the journey we all face—go out, discover, become lost, suffer, have a crisis, hunger, repent and gain hard wisdom, seek answers, grow, come to understanding. We all have a crucible. We all must conquer our fear. This is why you must always have new goals; you can never come to rest. Being static is the one sure way to dry up all the blessings God brings you; playing it safe is the sure way to bring on disaster. Nothing in nature is static, and neither should you be. You must remain hungry, keep striving, keep becoming.

We All Make a Different Journey

With all the diverse types of people on this planet, there is one fact we all have in common: we all make a journey where we pass from one state of being to another and are changed along the way. Every one of us has a different journey: marriages, jobs, troubles with drugs, crime, or poverty. You had to have those experiences before you can come to understand that the only true place for you is within you.

You will never find what you are looking for outside yourself. Young people seem particularly susceptible to the lie that truth can be found outside their skin. That's why they acquire endless objects, experiment with drugs and multiple sex partners and jump from job to job; they are constantly in a mode of search. This is the Law of the Journey:

AS LONG AS YOU SEARCH FOR WHAT YOU WANT
OUTSIDE YOURSELF, YOUR JOURNEY WILL NOT END.

When we become older, the wiser among us slowly realize that the endless search for gratification and self-definition outside of ourselves isn't . . . making . . . us . . . happy! Only then do we begin to turn inward, learn meditation, ask questions, look at our characters in the mirror and start finding the causes of our miseries and triumphs in our own minds and spirits. The journey is different for each of us, but its conclusion is always the same: if we are to find the divine power in us, we must let go of the outward and move inward to hear God's voice. People will disappoint you. Possessions will bore you. But once you find what you need within you, you will never disappoint yourself. Only then are you ready to truly experience the metaphysical.

If You Aspire, Inspire

The words "spirit" and "inspire" are related, as you can no doubt see. They share the Latin root "spir," which means "to breathe." That is the essence of manifestation: to breathe life and existence into that which was invisible, first manifesting it as thought, then as material presence.

Spirit is the essence of everything, and *inspiration* means "in spirit." You are not supposed to come into your money and success through perspiration, but through inspiration. That is the Spirit working through you, a willing and comprehending host, to create miracles and anointing. Inspiration is the act of imparting Spirit onto the physical world to cause effects—in your case, the physical manifestation of the God has decreed to be due to come into your life.

*Spirit is the essence of everything, and **inspiration** means "in spirit."*

Inspiration in the normal way of understanding—using people to inspire you, remind you of people who have achieved in a way you want to achieve, and remind you of your best self—is wonderful. But inspiration in the sense of Spirit is when you become an adept wielder of the power of "I Am," you go into the world and speak your declaration of what you are, and the thing comes to pass. Others are inspired by you and attracted to your purpose and power.

Discover the Heroic Angel in You

And the angel answering said unto him, I am Gabriel, that stand in the presence of God; and am sent to speak unto thee and to shew thee these glad tidings. And behold, thou shalt be dumb, and not able to speak, until the day that these things shall be performed, because thou believest not my words, which shall be fulfilled in their season.

— Luke 1:19-20

Gabriel means "mighty man of God, hero of God." Gabriel is the messenger of God, and he signifies man in his realization and demonstration of his "I Am" power. He is elevated to conscious and manifest oneness with God. He is a man who will rule the Universe.

Gabriel is pure Spirit, but he is also us. We have the same potential he does—to manifest an absolute oneness with God. Gabriel is not an angel outside of you, but the heroic power of "I Am" within you. God in you wants you to come forth as a hero. God wants you to demonstrate the holiness of your being.

Gabriel was an angel over angels; he was a master angel. In the same way, you can have mastery over your thoughts. You can also have master thoughts, the thoughts and patterns of thinking that control the thoughts under them. Once you have such master thoughts, you have evolved to a higher level of focus and control.

How can you manifest such an advanced level of control over your own thoughts? It takes time and practice, but here are some ways:

- Develop your meditation skills. Learn to quickly drop your mind into a still, quiet state that is a receiver for the Word of God.

- Develop the "habits" of your brain so that when you want something, the first place you look for it is not without, but within. How can you manifest what you want from your own will and inspiration?

- Only associate with people who follow the same upward path as you. The people you hang with will define who you are and where you are headed.

- Build your Spirit like a muscle by reminding yourself that you are the blessings you currently have in your life—your friends, your family, your possessions, your ideas.

When you have reached the point where you have evolved into a Gabriel in thought and mind, you will be a Presence. The dynamic presence of the Spirit of God permeates everything and forever makes itself known. That is the energy you will radiate, and it will enable you to command your thoughts to manifest in your material experience, and they will. That is the full potential for which you are intended.

* * *

SUMMARY

- You must surrender your mind to a higher power to get what you want.

- What you desire and aspire to is already in the earth, fully formed.

- Manifestation takes time.

- God will test you while you are waiting for manifestation.

- You won't be filled until you are hungry.

- We must all make a challenging journey to self-realization.

- If you look without for what you want, your search will not end.

- Inspiration is your power to create.

- You have a heroic angel within you.

Chapter 12

THE LAW OF ONENESS

———•———

When you come before God as a little child, open and excited and ready to go in any direction, that's when you discover the path God intends for you. So open your mind and find what excites you and stirs the passion in your belly. Intellect interferes with Spirit. It will compel you to ask God how it will be done, and that's none of your business. Be patient, be still and let God do His work. If you come to Him as a child and let yourself experience the wonder of Spirit and imagine all the possibilities that can manifest, you will call forth great things.

In the last chapter, we talked about your relationship and similarity to the archangel Gabriel, who appeared to Mary and told her she would become the mother of Jesus. In this chapter, we will explore further into the nature of Gabriel and look at how fully embracing the Gabriel within you will bring you into oneness with God.

Discover the Gabriel in You

God is waiting for you to discover and work the divine nature and heroism within you. To discover the Gabriel within you, you must stand in the presence of God. Gabriel is the messenger of peace and restoration, guardian of the sacred treasury. Gabriel is one of the exalted Spirits of God, a partner with God in shaping the Universe and guiding the passage of Man through the material world.

Your essence is no different from Gabriel's. The only thing that separates you is flesh. Gabriel's status as pure Spirit allows him to stand in the presence of God. But you are also Spirit walking around in a temporary cloak of flesh; that means you have the potential to stand before God as well. If you stand open to the Word of Spirit, you also stand in the presence of God. You are on a journey to become like Gabriel—a man of God, standing in the presence of God and claiming your divine nature. Angels are messengers of Spirit.

Gabriel signifies Man's realization of his "I Am" standing. In a very real way, Gabriel is man fully realized! God wants you to signify your "I Am" status and to manifest the power of your "I Am" nature as god. God wants you to manifest your power and stand with Him as god. To do this, you must become like Gabriel, a hero of God working fully in Spirit, with your intellect serving Spirit.

You are the fullest expression of God's Word in the world. God wants to make you ready to claim that birthright, stand in His presence and walk in anointing.

Is There a Gabriel in Your Life?

God will send you a messenger, a man of God, a Gabriel, to make you understand the vision that awaits you. There is a vision waiting for you. Are you ready to see it? God will sometimes bring you a man of God—a real person, not an angel—to show you what is about to come to you. This is your Gabriel, your messenger in flesh and Spirit, the harbinger of what is to come. Your Gabriel can take the form of anyone in your life: a friend, a pastor, a parent, a stranger.

Life occurs in its proper season, a season determined by God in His wisdom. Sometimes, you will be in a season of life where you have to be made to understand God's vision for you. That's why God will send a Gabriel to help you understand the vision. We all need help from time to time accepting what God is saying and interpreting the information of Spirit. That is where your Gabriel intercedes.

When You Create Access, You Gain Access

The truth about Gabriel illustrates a vital principle about the Universe:

MUCH OF WHAT YOU CAN ACHIEVE DEPENDS ON WHO AND WHAT YOU CAN ACCESS.

Access to people, power, influence, and most important, God, determines how far you can go, what comes to you, and how hard you have to work to manifest what you want. Some people are blessed with access. What you have access to—how much access you have to God—determines the quality of favor in your life.

Can you gain access to the people you need? That will always depend on how much access you create for others. If it's not clear already, let me restate: the Universe functions in an economy of *reciprocity*, in which what you send out comes back to you, usually multiplied. If you send out attention on the negative, negative people and actions will appear in your life. If you create access for others, access will come back to you in the same way. It is the ironclad rule of the cosmic economy, one that God Himself is bound to obey.

For example, I know about a financial advisor who, as his only business development effort, simply works to connect new people in the neighborhood with things they need that have nothing to do with finances: child care, contractors, and so on. He never says anything to them about financial planning or investments. Finally, when the time is right, he mentions that he's a planner, and the huge majority of these people give him their business. Why? Because he gave access without worrying about reward, and built trust as a result.

When you make connections between people without worrying about reward, more connections will come back to you.

I know of another financial advisor who was part of a church that was paying 12 percent on their mortgage, which is highway robbery. He sent the church leaders to a bank where they were able to refinance the church's loan for the church for five percent. Doing that saved the church hundreds of thousands of dollars, and the financial advisor got nothing in return. But when members of the congregation needed investment help in the future, who do you think got all their business? That's right.

Give and create access, and you will receive favor. When you make connections between people without worrying about reward, more connections will come back to you. Become a source of access! You will create wealth, trust, energy, possibility and favor. Be in the best interest of other people; don't see what you can get; see what you can give. Wisdom, ideas, guidance, advice, compassion and connections cost you nothing.

Know Your Destiny

You have a divine destiny to claim, one that has been set aside for you since the Creation: to stand at God's right hand and help Him shape the cosmos. That is your true destiny; all else is illusion or misperception. Your true destiny is to be co-creator with the Creator.

God in Mind and Spirit is without limit, but in creating the material plane of existence, He gave himself limits. He made Himself dependent on Man—on you—just as we are dependent on Him. Without God, you can do nothing in Spirit. Without you, God can do nothing in flesh. Ours is a relationship of mutual need. God works with man in order to bring about manifestation. You are God's junior partner!

This is a difficult idea for many to grasp. Some Christians, even those who are saved, are more comfortable with the idea of themselves as slaves of sin waiting for God to judge them. That's a comfortable fallback position, because it absolves you of making choices. It's the "apathy defense." And it's worthless. You will never achieve what you truly can achieve as long as you internalize the idea that you are *inferior to God.*

Until you can understand your true destiny, you are walking in a false destiny. Until you understand your core being, you will not understand your creation of being. Your true destiny is to be "I Am," to be a creator in Spirit who becomes the things he or she desires to manifest, then manifests them in physical reality. You will never lose weight if you say, "I have to lose weight." You will only lose weight when you say "I am thin" and I'm eating accordingly. You cannot achieve that which you've got to get. You can only achieve that which "I Am."

How Are You Shaping the World?

You have the incredible power to shape the world according to your thoughts and your vision. You doubt this, look at the work of man's hands: we create islands out of nothing, build bridges that connect countries, build tunnels under oceans. We're even changing the climate of this planet, for better or worse. All those changes began in the mind and Spirit of man. You have the power to move and inspire people just as God does. God works through you but also inspires you to work with your own power. How are you influencing people and things right now, with your thoughts?

Once you are in your destiny, God will work with you. If He is not working with you, you're out of sonship. You are not in "oneness." Let me take that a step further:

IF THE LORD IS NOT WORKING WITH YOU,
YOU ARE WORKING AGAINST HIM.

If you are not in alignment with your divine destiny, you are not using your power. You become an agent of negativity and ignorance. God can only enter into the earth through man. God needs you as much as you need him.

Are You the Water or a Wave?

To work with God, you must be the living Word of God, speaking the Truth of God. You must close the Bible and *be* the Truth of

God. Only then will God work through you. You have to go forth in your realization of "I Am" for God to confirm His work with signs and wonders. When you are being the Word and Truth of God, signs will appear to show you that God walks and works with you.

How do you become "I Am?" It's as simple and as cosmic as thought: you must *know* that you are the things and effects you seek. It's not enough simply to state "I Am" the house, the car, the bank account. What good is that if you don't actually believe it? You must know in your heart and Spirit that you already are those things—that you are what-ever you want to manifest, even though it does not yet appear in your visible experience. That's what God does. He *is* the things He creates; they exist in His mind long before He manifests them with His Word. You must do the same thing if you are to walk with God.

> *When you are being the Word and Truth of God, signs will appear to show you that God walks and works with you.*

God has a system that He has imposed on the Universe, and you cannot control the nature of that system. You do not control the Laws of Thinking; you can either choose to follow them or defy them. It's like inspiration and God's thought are an ocean that we are all part of. If you are riding in accordance with the movement of the ocean, then you are a smooth swell that rises and falls and moves where the ocean takes you. There is no turmoil or violence. But when we are not riding with the ocean of inspiration, we are waves. Waves are in turmoil with the ocean, the great source of inspiration. If you are divided from God, you are separated from that ocean. You are a wave about to crash onshore.

What matter is showing up in your life to separate you from the ocean of inspiration? What can you to do recapture that divine oneness with the Lord?

The Law of Oneness

You are meant to be at one with God. It's that simple. You were created by God; you are made of the same stuff as God, only pressed out into this world. Man is God pressed out into flesh. And as we age and gain in experience, we also often gain an inflated sense of self, a sense of "it's all me" that divides us from the natural inborn oneness that we should be experiencing with and in God. There is really no separation; we remain one with God in Spirit, but if we do not know it or accept it, it's as if we are separate. Oneness only matters when you can use it to manifest God's will in your life.

That is why God will sometimes make you still so He can work—so you can be in oneness. We think we know what is real, and what is God. But we rarely do. Our know-it-all intellects often get in the way of what is truly real. Sometimes, being dumb is the only way a person who hears a prophecy can walk through a season of uncertainty without doubt derailing the prophecy. As we have said in the past, when you question or doubt the prophecy, you drive it away from you; you separate yourself from oneness.

The Law of Oneness is this:

~

"I AM" REAFFIRMS YOUR ONENESS WITH GOD AND EMPOWERS YOU TO MANIFEST.

~

Give Peace a Chance

Breakthroughs are always there, always a thought away, if

only we can see them. When you are in turmoil, you cannot see the breakthrough that connects you with God's Word. But if you know it's there, you can be at peace, let the prophecy work, and see the breakthrough when the time is right.

Being one with God requires being at peace with yourself. Our minds are incredible instruments, but they are simultaneously our greatest asset and our greatest liability. The same machines of thought that enable us to conceive of and create wondrous things like space vehicles, operas and computers also clutter our minds with doubts, details, regrets, reminders, envy and ego. Our brains get noisy and busy and chaotic, and that din drowns out the voice of God trying to speak to us, to remind us of our divine nature. Here's a basic truth about God:

~

GOD NEVER RAISES HIS VOICE.

~

He doesn't need to. He doesn't want to. He's not interested in shouting to make you hear; He wants you to *want* to hear, to seek out His Word. To be able to hear Him, you must take action to quiet your mind and be at peace. Only then will you hear God speaking softly and firmly to your Spirit. Sometimes you must be at peace, meditate, and be in a place where even tough times cannot move you. Then you are in a position to let prophecy work.

This takes practice and trust. Many people are not comfortable "letting things happen." They want to provoke, force the action, and take steps. That is all well and good once you have things rolling, but it's no way to work with God. It's no way to manifest your "I Am." Being at peace and one with God means turning off that tendency to manipulate events and let the world flow around you. That opens God to work in you.

You should only have people around you who increase your peace. Those who don't will roil the waters of your mind and derail the work of God in yourself. If people do not bring you peace, they are not from God.

You should only have people around you who increase your peace.

What Is Inside Will End Outside

When you reach that sense of peace where God can speak and you can hear, you will reconnect with the oneness that is your birthright. When that occurs, whatever is happening internally in you will express itself externally. That is the nature of the Universe: all things begin internally, in the mind, and are expressed materially through the Spirit. You cannot find happiness outside yourself. You can only find it inward. If you spend all your time chasing possibility in the material world, you will be in desperation and want, and that is Hell.

You cannot achieve anything outside of yourself. Never marry someone because you are lonely, because you will still be lonely no matter what you do. You are only fit to marry someone when you love yourself first and foremost. Nothing outside of you can make you happy. Until you do not need anyone, you cannot be happy with anyone. If something outside of you can make you happy, it can make you unhappy. That's too much power to give away.

Only God should have the access to your happiness or unhappiness. If something is outside of God, it is an idol. Know this:

~

GOD WILL TEST EACH THING AND PERSON IN YOUR LIFE TO SEE IF IT IS AN APPOINTMENT OR A DISAPPOINTMENT.

~

If it's a disappointment, get rid of it. It is not of God. It has been placed there to lead you astray.

Let Them Find Their Own Path

The paradox of the Laws of Thinking is that even though you might inherit and master this knowledge, you cannot make anyone else master it. You have no choice but to let people find their own path and not try to protect them from their mistakes and pain. That is why God sets obstacles in your path and throws you curves when you become too comfortable: He knows that human beings learn their best lessons through hardship. If your path to happiness is within you, be generous enough to let others walk their own paths.

Is that selfish? No. What is selfish is not letting people be themselves, not letting them have their own journey. All people must make a journey and find the divine nature of God. They must have their own struggles and find their own way, even if it takes years and requires much suffering. You cannot change another person's Spirit. Not even God can do that. He is limited by His own Laws. A person can only transform his own mind and Spirit.

Look after your own Spirit and become an inspiration to others. Remember, walking in inspiration is the way to find what you love and your purpose under God. If we do not follow our inspiration, we wallow in desperation! Inspiration is imagination, the activity of the Spirit working on the mind. Desperation is the seed of need. If you don't get inspired and create, you will *become* desperation. Desperation is the lust of the flesh, and there is no satisfying that lust with material things, ever. Beware of becoming trapped in an endless cycle of material want.

You Were Meant to Sculpt Creation

God placed the power of Creation within you. He seeks to guide you to that power, but not to shape what you make with it. That is why you are a sovereign being, so you can continue God's work and shape the world with your own vision, as God shaped it with His. You are the heir to the creative power of God, if you embrace it.

When you accept this, you will find yourself to be most inspired when you are creating. You will only be happy when you are the creator. Creation will become addictive, part of your DNA, part of your daily bread and the breath of your life. That's why *recreation* should be pronounced "re-creation." You're always creating, even when you're playing. That's why sex is fun. It's *pro*-creation.

Life is not about comfort, but creation. You were mean to create restlessly, endlessly, to always be seeking new horizons. Why do we celebrate the restless minds of explorers and discoverers? It's not just because they create new technologies or find new species of animals. It's because they embody the best of us, that boundless creative Spirit with which God has gifted us. You are an explorer!

You are also a sculptor. The sculptor does not carve a shape out of stone; he sees the shape that's already inside the stone, then chisels away everything that isn't that shape. He molds the stone by his perception. The movements of his hands and hammer are incidental, inevitable. When you are one with God, that is what you can do.

Summary

- There is a Gabriel in your life with a message for you.

- To gain access, you must create it.

- You have a divine destiny to be one with God.

- You will only hear God when your mind is at peace.

- You cannot find happiness outside yourself.

- Everyone must walk his own path to awareness.

- You are a sculptor of creation.

Chapter 13

THE LAW OF PREDESTINATION

———✦———

So far, we've emphasized how much of manifesting what the Universe has in store depends on you. But don't make the mistake of leaving God out of the picture. God must be behind everything you do, or you will steer onto the rocks. God is the guiding, driving force—the sublime vision behind all human activity. If you're not following God's vision, you're following your own earthly vision, and that will by its nature be of the flesh and it will be corrupt!

In order for people to obey God's law, there must be a revelation. When people do not accept divine guidance, they run wild. Without God's purpose and vision, there is no rudder. People cannot see, and they end up going in any direction. Whenever a culture is oppressing a people, they will remove the seers or prophets from within their midst. That is a hallmark of every oppressive society from the time of Jesus to Nazi Germany, which expelled or executed all the artists and intellectuals in its midst. Seers and visionaries are the eyes of the people. Without them, the people are blind and it becomes easier to lead them away from God.

Where there is ignorance of God, crime runs wild, vice is rampant and society does not advance. There is no central mission, no path toward the light. There is only chaos. People perish in Spirit without a redemptive revelation of God. So it is vital for you to be able to recognize when a vision is from God and when it is not. The way you can test whether a vision is from God or not is if it has a redemptive element in it. If it does not, it is not godly. Your vision or prophecy from God will have a component that promises to lead you toward Spirit and your full realization of self as god. God will never send you anything that will lead you away from Him; God's vision always has hope embedded within it. If it does not, cast it away from you!

Cancer Is Contagious

As you can see, walking the path toward one's own divinity means balancing the need to declare one's "I Am" status and become what one wants with being obedient and receptive to the vision of God. That is not an easy path to walk, and all of us have overbalanced and fallen at one time or another.

If you have fallen short, you must do something that can be quite difficult: look at the ways you have brought something into your life that is pulling you away from God. If you want to know what's in you, look at what's outside of you. Sometimes, this discovery can be quite painful, because you have to see what you have done. You have to take responsibility for the choices you have made and what those choices have brought to your doorstep: bad people, poor opportunities, crime or other misfortunes. It's important to deal with the pain of looking at what you have done, because only then can you reject the people who are infecting your life.

Never let someone pass their cancer on to you. Cancer of the Spirit is a contagious disease. It infects you with negative thoughts, defeatism, and cynicism about what you can accomplish and about what God has in store for you. No one makes choices for you; you make your own choices. You are responsible. You produce the effects that appear in your life, and those set you on your course. Be courageous enough to look around and see the cancers growing in your world. Then cut them out and move on. They are not your concern. Remember this always:

YOU ARE CALLED TO GIVE AND HELP OTHERS, BUT
YOU CANNOT HELP THOSE WHO REFUSE TO SEE.
THEY WILL ONLY DRAG YOU DOWN WITH THEM.

The Dangers of Ego

Why would some people wish to drag you down and pull you away from God? Because once you become aware of your divine, highest self, you become a danger because you can go forth and accomplish everything. There are people who are from the devil, who have a self-interest in keeping you ignorant of your divinity, unaware of your "I Am," either because that gives them temporal power over you in this world, or because they fear the implications of you coming to God and achieving success, because this will remind them of what they have failed to do. Awareness makes you dangerous to those who are unaware.

The rich are aware of who and what they are and have an objective in mind. The poor are not. Prophecy is about awakening people's awareness of their higher self and God's intentions. But just as everything is a balancing act, once you are awake to your higher self, you must carefully avoid the traps of ego. Ego is a wily serpent and has been around much longer than you; the tricks of ego are subtle and avoiding them takes keen perception and much meditation.

Understand: God has an ego. All sentient beings do. Part of the purpose of ego is to remind us of our worth and power. But ego walks a fine line, and when you cross that line into thinking that you know more than the Father, you derail your own train. You must let go of ego on your journey to full spiritual realization. Ego is your ugly silent partner.

Ego stands itself up against the mind and purpose of God. It is your intellect fighting for primacy versus God. Ego can even win; God will not stop it from winning. But with ego in charge, you will not connect with the God that resides inside you. The letters "e-g-o" even mean other things:

~

EASING GOD OUT.

EARTH GUIDE ONLY.

ETCHING GOD OUT.

~

Have the Right Kind of Pride

You are always doing a dance of duality with your ego self, and that dance keeps you from God. You cannot be split into two people, two selves—a being of Spirit and a being of intellect. You must put your intellect at the service of your Spirit. Then God in you will arise and you will move in Spirit.

154

When you do that, your enemies (also called your "inner me"s) will arise. They will show their hands and you can cast them out. The God in you will come forth and you will speak with God's voice. God will be able to work through you.

Ego is like a barrier that prevents God from giving you what you want. Once it's gone, God can get busy.

> *Ego is like a barrier that prevents God from giving you what you want.*
>
>

That brings up the subject of pride. Pride gets a bad rap in most traditional religious thinking—pride goeth before a fall and all that. Pride is one of the Seven Deadly Sins. Yet there is nothing wrong with the right kind of pride, the pride that makes you refuse to fail, that makes you take care of your body, that drives you to succeed. That's "positive pride." Negative pride comes when you cannot let go of ego and hand God the tiller of your ship.

You must have humility before God to allow Spirit to take over, yet take pride in the fact that you are God's co-creator and work in His vision. Again, we see the importance of *balance* in living a life as co-Creator! When you live only in pride, it means you really don't want to know what the spirit realm is saying. You are only interested in what the physical realm is telling you. In this way, you can have the nature of God but not operate in that nature.

When you want to do things your own way, you become separate from your true nature. You separate yourself from God. When you want to assert your own ideas over the vision of God, ego is in control. Let ego go, and God in you will arise. Your ego deafens you to the prophecy of God in your Spirit. Let ego go and you can hear God's voice speaking in your Spirit. You and God are reunited, and it feels so good!

155

Don't Get Stuck in Desire

You must be diligent in your focus and attention on what you want to manifest. You will only become rich when you become diligent. It's equally important not to let yourself be stuck in desire. We have talked about desire before, and you know that having a desire to manifest something is the first step to bringing it into corporeal existence. That's fine, but what you must not do is get *stuck* in desire—be so preoccupied with your desire that you don't do the work needed to make it manifest. Desire is slothful. When a person is stuck in desire, it means they are lazy. Diligence and consistent work are the keys. The soul of the diligent will be made fat, while the soul of the desirous person will starve.

Diligence means you have found something worth focusing on, worth respecting, so you stick with that thing over time and bring it into manifestation patiently and steadily. Miracles rarely occur in instants; they take years.

Pay respect to get respect. Discover the things you want to manifest and pay respect to them by keeping a laser-sharp focus on them. That same respect will be paid by others as they work to help you manifest your goals. When you become diligent, you attract people who can help you. The diligent man is worthy of the company of kings. When you do a sloppy job, you will be in the company of obscure, mean men.

Be Able to Walk Away

This all means that you must have the insight and depth of discernment to choose your goals and leave behind the things and people that are not your goals or do not serve your goals. You must be able to *walk away*. Read and remember this maxim:

⁓

WALKING AWAY FROM SOMETHING MEANS YOU HAVE MASTERED IT.

⁓

If you can walk away from a thing or a person, you can let it go. It no longer has power over you; you have power over it. Walking is a sign of mastery. Jesus walked everywhere, you know. Running is a sign of desperation. Masters do not need to hurry; they know all good things flow from them and will wait for their due time. Walking in Spirit means you are not living to fulfill the pleasures of the flesh. Walking is moving by mind, not by instinct. That is your higher nature running the show, not your appetite.

What all the material in this chapter is calling you to do is develop wisdom, awareness and the kind of incisive perception that is the hallmark of Spirit. Prophets have this kind of perception, where they see not only the things but the *significances* of the things. They can perceive not only what something is but what it *means*. That is a time-honored mode of thought that you must master before you can fully benefit from the Laws of Thinking.

What I am asking is that you set yourself on a path to be wise as the serpent. Forget the biblical accounts of the serpent as the devil; that's not what we're talking about. Instead, think of the nature of a serpent. The serpent does not run. It focuses on its prey, waits until the right moment, then strikes. Never move in haste. Masters operate in wisdom.

Moses' walking stick was turned into a serpent when he confronted Pharaoh with God's command that the Hebrews be set free from bondage, and when the magicians of the Egyptian court also turned their staves into snakes, Moses' devoured them.

Why? Because Moses' focus was greater than all of theirs. Being wise as serpents means to have the focus of the serpent. If you can wait on what you desire long enough, it will lay itself before you because you have been diligent in your thoughts.

What You Desire Is Already Waiting for You

Desire starts the engines of the Universe to begin manifesting, stating that "I Am" and becoming that which you seek starts the wheels and gears turning, and diligent focus keeps the engine running hot and clean. But in reality, what you desire is already in existence; the flow of time that carries you with it simply has not reached the thing yet.

Your ambition is your real creed. What you desire is your true nature. Not your words, not even your thoughts reflect who you really are. We are what we desire. What do you want? Do you want the physical, the stuff of this world, or of the Spirit? That defines not only who you are but where you are headed.

If you know you deserve something, it shall be granted. If you can get to the place where you master and control what you want, it will come to you. Desire etches it in clay, and the world manifests it in stone. But you must know that you deserve what you desire. Remember, doubt or a word can abort your vision while it is still in the womb. Here's a stunning fact:

~

WE ALWAYS GET WHAT WE DESERVE.

~

Did something bad happen to you and you protested, "But I go to church and I'm a good person, I didn't deserve this!" Yes you did, because something in your words or thoughts brought it to you. We all get what we deserve, anointment or disappointment. You must be full of the feeling of deservedness for what you want or it will not manifest. At the same time, you must banish thoughts about what you do not deserve, or you will inadvertently attract misfortune to yourself. Each passionate wish draws your blessing nearer.

Wrapped in Silence and Unseen

In *The Miracle of Right Thought*, we read that what we desire to manifest is already waiting for us; we just cannot perceive it yet. We have not done the work needed to bring it into our experience yet. But that does not make it any less real. That is why you must train your mind and Spirit to focus, walk in power, and listen at peace to God.

The things you crave wait in the distance. They have *always* been waiting for you to attract them to you. This is the Law of Predestination:

∼

WHAT YOU'RE WAITING FOR IS REALLY
WAITING FOR YOU.

∼

The things you were meant by God to have—the wealth, the house, the business, the life you want—have always been in existence, and right now they are sitting at the other end of the linear timeline that we all walk, waiting for you to become passionate about them and attract them to you. The future is the destination for all of us, and that destination has already been determined by God. It's literally "pre-destination." Even more, you have always *known* that's where you were *meant* to go. Once you awaken to your destination, it is waiting for you to know that you deserve it and to become it! You cannot attract it to you until you become it! Shout "I Am!"

This is an incredible idea. Your highest aspirations and dreams have already taken shape in the realm of Spirit, created before Time so that they are not bound by the limitations of time, as you are in the physical realm. Just as God created all that is and will be in His mind before He ever brought it into physical manifestation with the Word, everything you desire is down the road in Time, waiting for you to bring it into existence with your Word . . . when you're ready.

Your highest aspirations and dreams have already taken shape in the realm of Spirit . . .

Because before you can manifest it, you must have the perception to know what it is and name it. You cannot create something if you don't know its nature. Naming, as I said before, has great power. Once you can become the thing you want (self-insight) and name the thing you are trying to bring to you (insight about your goals) you will be able to attract the unseen and bring it into material existence. You will become like a planet with a gravitational pull that only attracts success, good people and blessings.

Something Great Is Trying to Get to You

What you want is wrapped in silence and unseen until you have the faith and passion and Spirit to make it visible and audible. Until you can perceive in Spirit, you cannot perceive what is waiting for you. It has your voice and your form, and it belongs to no one else. God has decreed that it is yours, and He will not transfer the title to anyone else. But you have to claim it.

Something great is trying to get to you. Live worthy of what you want and it shall come. Live in Spirit, without fear.

* * *

SUMMARY

- God's revelation will always be redemptive.
- The cancer of other people is contagious.
- Ego blocks God's intent for you.
- You must be humble enough to let God take the wheel.
- Being stuck in desire is slothful; desire, then get to work.
- You always get what you deserve.
- What you desire is already waiting for you, silent and unseen.

Chapter 14

THE LAW OF HUMILITY

———

We've talked a little about humility, about the importance of surrendering the ego and letting God take the wheel of your actions and drive your thoughts. But the concept of letting go of ego, of balancing pride and suppression of pride, is such a complex one that we're going to get more deeply into it. In fact, we're going to talk about the Law of Humility and how it can help you open yourself completely to what God wants to serve up to you.

What is humility? It's the suppression of the ego and the submission to God's Word. You see, God does not have the ability to force His will upon you; that's not how the Laws work. He can bring things into or take things out of your life, but you always have choice. Remember, you are part of God's substance; you possess the power to thwart His will concerning you. Of course, if you do that you will manifest misery and hardship in your life, but it is your choice. On the other hand, your ability to bend before God's will gives Him the ability to raise you up. Your ability to lie down gives God the ability to lift you up. Your intellect and ego anchor you to the earth, while letting go of those heavy weights frees you to operate in the realm of Spirit.

163

God Favors Humility

Remember when we spoke about favor, and the concept that favor is not fair? Favor chooses those who operate in God's system, not necessarily those who appear to deserve favor for the acts they perform on earth. Your goal is to be a "Favor-ite" of God. And God favors humility, not baseless pride. Notice that word: *baseless* pride. God does not penalize pride in you for the kind of person you are, for your honesty, your kindness and your love. Those are qualities in which you should take pride. No, God penalizes the kind of pride that has no reason, pride that refuses to acknowledge that God's wisdom and knowledge of the workings of the Universe far exceeds what yours will ever be. Pride is your mind trying to be God. Do that and God will·clam up. You'll never hear a word.

> *Pride is your mind trying to be God. Do that and God will clam up. You'll never hear a word.*

God gives you the grace to let go of your pride. God favors humility, not pride. As a bishop in my church, I'm called a "prince of the church," which is a title that could engender baseless pride in any man. But I can't have that. My standing as bishop can only serve to remind me that my awareness of God's voice is intended to give me humility. I have grace so I can be humble, not so I can be proud. In fact, it takes great pride to be able to humble yourself and not lose yourself. You can only be humble without resentment when you truly know who you are!

The Law of Humility is this:

~

GOD RESISTS THE PROUD, BUT GIVES GRACE TO THE HUMBLE.

~

Submit to God and the Devil Loses You

Submit to God and you resist the devil. Obedience to God's Word and will, opening your Spirit to God's Word and living in prophecy and Spirit, not placing your own intellect over God's word—these guarantee that the devil will have no hold on you. God will exalt you and give you favor.

God wants you to be penitent and mourning. He wants you to be like Christ: He wants you to inflict yourself and grieve, to let your old self, old life and old state of mind die. He wants you to grieve over that dead life then be raised up by Him into a life of Spirit. This is the truth God wants you to come into, but can you see it is only accessible if you are willing to let your old self go? It is impossible to surrender so completely if your pride tells you that your old life and your old wisdom are superior to God's.

This is a constant struggle and mystery. The ways of God are subtle and complex; after all, He has had eternity to work on them, and He knows what gets results. You have had a few decades, and you have not had the benefit of watching billions of human lives play out so you can see what actions result in triumph and which ones produce tragedy. Everyone has a due time for exaltation. The trick is knowing the due time. While you're waiting for that time, you must humble yourself.

Grace is God's unmerited favor toward you. To be a "Favorite," you must be a "Humble-ite." You must give up ego. You must place yourself in God's hand, so that when He lifts His hand He lifts you with it. If you must have pride (and you will) your pride should be pride in your humility and in working in unison with God's purpose.

The Wisdom of the Elders

God can be a tough taskmaster, but let's face it, it's only because we are so lazy. Human beings waste much of our potential and laze along not really working very hard until there is a crisis. Then we act and become inspired. So God deals in crisis—physical, emotional and spiritual. He's a master motivator—the Tony Robbins of the cosmos! God knows that when we're comfortable, we're lazy, and we become inert. So if He favors us, he rarely lets us get too comfortable, amen.

The Lord loves it when we live in humility but also live out on the edge. In other words, when we submit to God's direction, then take enormous risks to bring that direction to fruition. He also is pleased when young people yield to the wisdom of their elders. Elders are wise because they have seen many lives play out, and they know that human behavior falls into patterns. If you listen, they can teach you how to start seeing the patterns in your life and in others' lives. Say you can't seem to find a man or a woman who treats you right, but you don't know why? An elder might talk to you for a few minutes and say, "Son, you keep choosing the same kind of woman. Can't you see the pattern?" And suddenly the pattern will be clear; when you're too close to it, it looks the same as the rest of the wall.

And if you are an elder, listen up: God wants you to share your wisdom with younger people. It's part of your responsibility as a child of God and as a co-creator. Like a boss at a company who explains to new employees what the company's policies are, you are called to impart wisdom to young minds who will hear it. You have seen much in your life; you have seen the patterns play out, seen young people who are humble and brave and others who are prideful, fearful and foolish. Foolishness is part of youth; children are God's fools, after all. But when young Spirits will listen, you must enlighten them.

Explain to them not why they should listen to you, but why they should listen to God. Remind them that no matter what any doctrine tells them, they are part of God, and are destined to use their divine ability to shape this world in hope. Remind them that focus, a meditative mind and a bold, courageous vision are all-powerful. Not all will listen to you—it's also a hallmark of the young that they rarely listen to their elders. Remember, you cannot tell anyone anything. But that doesn't mean you should not try. From one generation's reluctant students will come the next generation's willing teachers.

God Opposes the Willful

Put on the clothing of a servant and strip away your pride. Walk in the garb of the servant every day. It reminds you that you are subservient to another. It keeps you humble. It makes you walk in humility and frees you from pride and arrogance. That's good, because God sets himself against the proud, the willful, the overbearing, the boastful, and opposes, frustrates and defeats them. He takes pleasure in doing this, because in being proud and willful, they are scorning God and placing their wisdom above His.

You, too, will be scorned by those who feel you are misguided in your obedience to God. People who do not understand will mock you, try to turn you aside from your path, and tempt you to act in pride. That's okay. We need our scorners to make mockery of us so we will stay humble and God can reward us for our humility. God wants you to stay humble. You must learn to have peace while they are scorning you.

In the end, God scorns the scorners and gives his favor to the wise and humble. The wise shall inherit glory and shame shall be the reward of self-confident fools. You must bow to be humble and be willing to look a fool! Your ego must die daily even as your Spirit gains strength!

Be Worthy of What You Want

Whew! That's a tall order. But once you understand that in being humble before God you are actually becoming exalted in the real economy of this world, you will thrill to the idea. You will feel worthy of great things, and you will be. Because you cannot get what you desire until you live in a way that's worthy of it.

You must desire something, then move forward and live a life worthy of that ambition. Your ambition is your "I Am." If you can think about things that have hurt you, you can think about past victories, too. You can remember, "I Am that." It must be done already in your mind. More important, in your mind you must already be the person that you must *become* to deserve your ambition! That self already exists in the future, but you must meet that future self to bring all this into reality. The passion of your wish brings fulfillment closer. The feeling brings forth the result.

You can be infinite money if you can cultivate infinite desire and become infinite possibility. You must say, "I Am that!" You must live worthy of what you desire. Take the risk, dress your consciousness, become the thing that you want to be. Instead of buying the fake Rolex, buy the real Rolex even if you cannot afford it, and the self that is worthy of that wealth will come. You will call to it. Live rich and you will be rich!

Long before I lived in a mansion, I was the mansion. My wife was the mansion. We both felt it, experienced it in our minds and our Spirits before it manifested in our experience. We felt the soft beds, saw the soaring ceilings, walked the grounds in our imaginations and said, "Yes, this is what I am. This will be because it already is." And when the time came for the mansion that I live in now to manifest in our material world, nothing could stop it—not credit, lenders, construction permits, nothing. One thing worth learning:

WHEN THE TIME IS RIGHT FOR SOMETHING TO MANIFEST, IT IS UNSTOPPABLE.

The only one who can halt a manifestation is you, by turning away your attention and diligent focus or by allowing fear and doubt to kill the manifestation before it can become complete. What we yearn for, earnestly desire and strive to bring about tends to become a reality. When you yearn for it strongly enough, when you can feel and taste and experience it, you earn it. Yearning is earning!

That's your doctorate in *earnology*—you must earn what you desire in consciousness. Feel it before it comes to you, because it is already out there.

Your Dominant Thought

Thoughts have a hierarchy, just as angels do in Heaven. In fact, as we said in a previous chapter, words and thoughts are angels.

They are organized the same way: there are dominant angels and there are subordinate angels, and there are dominant and subordinate thoughts. Your mind will have many thoughts careening around in it; the key is, can you designate one dominant thought or pattern of thoughts that drives all the others? This is a skill you must master.

Whatever your innermost dominant thought is focused upon is what you will attract, move toward or become.

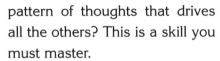

Your dominant thought becomes a sort of "safety net" that drives your thinking—and therefore what you attract to yourself—in a consistent direction. For example, if you are fundamentally a positive, confident person, even if you have a bad day you will tend to recover and think, "I can move on from this, and I will rise above it." Your dominant thought is one of success and overcoming obstacles. By the same token, if you are fundamentally a victim, even when good things happen you will see someone else as the cause and not give yourself credit. Your dominant thoughts can empower you or cripple you, and they will manifest according to their type.

Whatever your innermost dominant thought is focused upon is what you will attract, move toward or become. You must learn to focus your thought like a laser on your purposeful goals, objectives and action steps, in order to achieve the goals God has ordained for you.

Your Ideas Foreshadow the Future

If you remember high school English, you remember the literary concept of *foreshadowing*: using a subtle story element to hint at a larger story element still to come. Well, since the events and things that you will manifest in your consciousness already exist farther down the stream of Time than you can see now, your ideas are foreshadowings of things to come in your life.

That is faith—the substance of things hoped for and the evidence of things unseen. It doesn't make sense, but that doesn't make it any less true. In a very real way, the most advanced intellect is not the one that adheres to visible, provable physical laws and principles, but the one that can make an intuitive leap to a system that does not have empirical evidence behind it—but has the evidence of thousands of years of human experience. The science of the Laws of Thinking is the science of the mind and Spirit. Those are its laboratories and test tubes. You are its researchers.

All your ideas are a foreshadowing of a prophecy that is about to come. When you desire something with all your heart, you begin to establish a relationship with it. This is mysticism. When you have an idea or vision, your faith makes it real. So your ideas, crazy-sounding though they may be, are truly harbingers of what is to come. Entrepreneurs and inventors know this; it's why they can easily become obsessed and consumed by bringing an idea from the mind to some form of higher expression like a design or a business plan. When an idea is grounded in faith, you can't get it out of your head. It's an energy source and it must be expressed. When you can stay up all night writing or composing music or designing a new computer program, you're running on pure faith and your idea is drawing nearer each second.

We Must Live in the Ideal

You can see how faith, humility and dominant thoughts that drive your mind inexorably toward a positive destination must become reflexive if you're ever to really work with God to build the world you dream. That is why it takes years to learn to truly listen to God and get your mind and Spirit to a place where you can get out of your own way and let God roll up His sleeves and go to work. There are so many disciplines to master that the Laws of Thinking are like a martial art; in the end, to use it well, you must not be thinking at all. The method must be part of who you are.

The same applies here. To genuinely be "I Am" in your fullest divinity, you must cease "trying" to show humility and focus your dominant thought and have faith. You must internalize them all. This must all become like breathing to you, automatic and effortless. When you can do that, you are living in what we call the ideal. You are living with your mind focused not on what is, but on what *will be*.

We live too much in the material side of life, and not enough in the ideal. You don't want live too much in the physical, unless you want to establish a relationship with your house. Your house isn't going to bring you visions of the new things you can do. Your car isn't going to present you with new challenges that elevate you to a higher level of skill. You should establish a relationship with the Word. Only God and His Word can propel you along from one anointing to the next.

Something else to learn and master:

UNTIL YOU ESTABLISH A RELATIONSHIP WITH THE THING YOU WANT, IT CANNOT BECOME FLESH IN YOUR EXPERIENCE.

And how do you have a relationship with someone or something? You know it. You communicate with it. You understand it and have shared experience. Living in the ideal is reaching out into the future with your mind and knowing that things are coming, and then working with those things as if they are in your experience. So you can design the addition for your house before you own it, plan the trip in your boat before you find it, hire people for your business before you start it, and so on. Only by having that relationship with what you want will it come to you.

Live Young, Be Young

Learn to live mentally in the ideal that you wish to make real. To keep young, live in the mental state of youth. Passion, purpose and a love of life have kept people alive for decades who otherwise broke every rule of staying healthy! That is why people of will and passion live longer than negative people who might exercise five times a week. You are a being of spirit, not of flesh. You can be physically thin and spiritually fat.

To be beautiful, live in the mental state of beauty. Living in the ideal means all imperfections are eliminated. Ugliness, decrepitude and poverty do not exist in the ideal. This gives us a pattern for the perfection for which we are striving.

* * *

SUMMARY

- God favors the humble.

- Listen to the wisdom of your elders.

- If you are an elder, you are called by God to share your wisdom.

- God opposes the prideful and willful.

- You must live worthy of what you want.

- When the time is right for something to manifest, it cannot be stopped.

- Your ideas foreshadow what is to come.

- You must live in the ideal as if you already have a relationship with what you want.

Chapter 15

THE LAW OF FAITH

———◆———

What have you asked for? More important, if you don't ask for something, why should you expect to receive it? Asking is proof of humility. It puts you in the position of a child. Children know that if they ask, they shall receive. Why would God give us the ability to ask for something if we could not receive it? Asking is part of acting in faith, and that is the subject of this chapter.

Asking is having faith in the mighty ability of God. When you ask, it is an admission of limitation, and we already know that God is pleased by humility that admits He is the source of all things. It's important to ask in God's name; by doing so, you are encouraging God to keep creating new things. Asking is like lowering interest rates; it stimulates the cosmic economy.

Many times we don't receive things in life because we don't ask. There's a story about a man, just a few years ago, who decided to travel around the country practicing what he called "audacious asking": he didn't have any money, he just asked people for what he needed, like food and shelter. In almost every

175

case, when he asked, people provided. People are quick to open their hearts and homes to those who understand the power of asking. God is the same way.

Be as a Little Child

Ask and it shall be given you. But asking can be humiliating. It's humbling, and we know the need for humility in the face of God. If you cannot ask, what in you doesn't allow you? Is it pride? Fear? God will not reject you if you ask; He wants to be asked, because asking is a tacit acknowledgement of His place as provider of all blessings.

If you are going to be great, you must become as a child.

Children get it. Children ask for everything, and if Mom says no, what do they do? Right, they ask Dad. Children don't give up, because they don't hear "No." The only answer they will accept is "Yes." If you are going to be great, you must become as a child. Let go of your pride, ask, keep asking, and expect the answer to be "yes." Knock and keep knocking.

So much of operating in the system of God is about persistence, never quitting. Keep on! Press on and don't worry about the answer. Know that you deserve what you're asking for. Children always feel they deserve what they're asking for, but adults often do not. We must become as a child and keep asking. Behind every "no" is a "yes." Your boldness will only come forth when you believe you have a right to what you ask for. You must *know* that you are worthy of something, know that it is already yours when you ask for it. Because here's something to think about:

~

YOU'RE REALLY ASKING FOR SOMETHING THAT HAS ALWAYS BEEN YOURS TO BEGIN WITH.

~

What you want already exists in imagination down the time stream from you, and asking brings it closer. When you know something is yours, when you ask for it, and when you become that thing, you will manifest it.

Get Your Mind in Training

We all have bad habits that have made our minds flabby and lazy, and part of becoming masterful in the Laws of Thinking is getting your mind in shape. You must train your mind to be a spiritual worker in God's economy. Train your mind to focus on love, happiness and success and your mind will drive your habits. The more conditioned your thoughts are to see the world of material and Spirit, with infinite positive possibilities, the more you will move toward the things you want.

Train your mind for the good and positive, and your mind will not be able to move in the negative direction. What you try to persistently achieve, you tend to achieve. Express what you are persistent about. Express in your thoughts and speech what you want to achieve: prosperity, health, wealth and happiness.

Train your mind not to even acknowledge the possibility that things could turn out any other way. In this way, you make the blessings of your life a *fait accompli*—something already done and accomplished. The laws of the Universe have no choice but to respond in your favor. They have to operate the way they do, just like gravity.

THE LAWS OF THINKING

The Universe is God's economy, and your mind and your thoughts are your investment capital to build the future that God has in mind for you. You make them work for you; make them grow like investments with compound interest, with persistent thought and focus on the things you wish to manifest. What you visualize your desire in your mind with laser focus will drive your actions and allow you to operate from the Spirit. You will be working in prophecy. You spend your thoughts and purchase the wealth and prosperity you aspire to. Intensity and persistence of desire increases the power to realize your dreams. Energy must be strong, but also constant. Constancy of focus and intention is everything.

Passivity: The Sin of Inaction

The flip side of constant focus and fierce passion for what you wish to manifest is passivity. Passivity is a sin in the eyes of God, because it tells Him that you do not want to exert any effort or risk anything to achieve what you want; you just want it placed in your lap. That doesn't work for God; in His economy, the only things that have value are those that are earned. If you sit back and wait for things to come to you, you leave them in stasis in the world of Spirit. You paralyze God's ability to express His intentions through you. That is sinful.

Indifference is your enemy. It's a common disease in the Christian community, and it's contagious. Too many people are passive—they say they will have "whatever God wants me to have." That is foolishness. God does not decide what you will have; God decides what you *can* have. He places the table before you, but you must decide what to put on your plate. If you don't step up, and you end up going hungry and starving your soul, is that God's fault? No! He's not responsible for feeding you; you must feed yourself. You're not a child.

You cannot cede responsibility for what you want to God, because He's not responsible for manifesting what is in store for you. He's already decreed that it is yours, but you have to go get it. You must decide what you want and what you are, and vigorously and tenaciously go after it. God creates it, but you must want and claim it. People excuse failure as ""God's will." That is the vilest of lies: a lie to oneself. God's will determines your *potential*; your will determines whether or not you achieve it! You cannot be a good Christian sitting back on your behind, because you will *end up behind*—left in the wake of those who understand that God's purpose in you is for you to go out and create through your Spirit, to take what is meant for you. That is why God is an action, not simply a noun.

Minimization, Exaggeration, Infatuation, and Resentment

You should always be transacting business with the Almighty. Fear is what prevents you from doing so. And fear typically manifests in one of four ways: Minimization, exaggeration, infatuation and resentment.

- **Minimization**—We minimize people, places, ideas and events by representing them as having the least degree of importance or value. Minimization is a lie you tell yourself to make yourself believe that the things you want are not important enough to strive for. It is a buffer against failure and a terrible expression of doubt and lack of self-confidence.

- **Exaggeration**—We exaggerate about people, places, events and ideas by magnifying thing out of proportion and beyond truth. We distort in this way and often make small failures seem huge and make tiny barriers appear insurmountable. By exaggerating the things we face in life, we give ourselves a ready-made excuse for failure, or we psych ourselves out before we ever get started.

- **Infatuation**—When we become infatuated with something, we play up its positives and minimize its negatives. In this way, we can convince ourselves to become enamored of things that are not God, things outside us that do not serve our ultimate goals.

- **Resentment**—Resentment is the mirror image of infatuation, in which we exaggerate the bad things about a person, place or event to the point where all we see is the negative. Resentment can blind us to what is worthwhile about a person or opportunity; it is a lie we often tell ourselves to explain why we don't go after something we want (the "I didn't want that anyway" syndrome).

These four modes of thought are lies, and lies imprison your mind. When you are in prison, you cannot own property. Your rights are taken away. But God will only give you something when you hold the title deed to it. You must face the lies you tell yourself and free yourself of them before you can take title to what is yours!

The Generation of Lies

The lies you tell to others don't do anywhere near as much damage as the lies you tell yourself. Self-deceit breaks the machinery that connects you to Spirit; it paralyzes your will and makes it impossible for you to become the things you want. Lies are built-in excuses for failure, and as such, they are the doubts that will kill your vision before it ever starts to manifest.

There is a law to the spread of lies. Here is how the generation of lies progresses:

- The first lie births a generation of seven lies (or exaggerations or minimizations) that sustain and cover the first lie. In other words, when you lie to yourself or others you create an alternate reality that must be kept evolving with lies. Lies are its energy source! Can you imagine living in a world where the energy source was lies? But people do it every day.

- The 7 lies birth a generation of 49 lies.

- These 49 lies birth a generation of 343 lies, 7 for each.

- Those 343 lies birth a generation of 2,201 lies, and so on.

It's a bit like the roll call of the descendants of Adam and Eve in the Bible—only much less positive. This ever-growing legion of lies blots out the Light from on High that connects you to the Power within you. It is a legion of fallen angels that separate you from God.

Lies feed on lies. When you lie, you must create more lies to sustain the lie, to cover the false circumstances you have called into being. For example, if you lie to someone about a business deal that you had no intention of following through on, you must then make up a lie to explain why you did not do as you promised . . . then you must cover that lie with another. What's more, others spread your lies as they tell them to other people, so your lies have an exponential power to spread and multiply, like vermin. Lies truly are a pestilence; they are a plague that will afflict your life just as the plagues that afflicted Egypt during the time of Moses, brought on by the lie of slavery. Only when Moses brought to truth of God's freedom to the Hebrews did the plague end for the Egyptians.

Do You Have the Look?

We're learning that so much of having the things you want and manifesting what God has in store for you depends on knowing that you deserve that thing and indeed that you already are that thing. Well, another aspect to success is looking the part. It is difficult to *know* you are already a millionaire if you do not feel and look like one!

Remember, the most dominant thought is the one that gets played in life.

Wealth is a look. Success is a look. Poverty is a look. Everything has a look. You need the right look to produce the right results. Your physical look is a silent word speaking to the cosmos, telling it what you are. If you are still working on being able to maintain a strong, focused thought pattern that brings forth what you want, at least your look, style, speech and attitude can speak to Spirit and be working for you.

Remember, the most dominant thought is the one that gets played in life. Your mind should always be "up-reaching," elevating itself toward what is powerful, confident, strong, good and giving. The vibration of your mind must elevate in order to avoid manifesting that which you don't want in your life. You will draw what your mind focuses on into your experience. Elevation of thought will elevate your whole life to higher levels.

This is why it is so vital to always be asking those HOTS— Higher Order of Thinking questions about who you are and where you are going. You must always be seeking new stimuli to keep your mind and your passions on an upward path, away from distraction and toward creation. Over the years of practicing these Laws, your mind should develop and evolve to more easily scale the heights of positive, productive thought. The effort should become less, the rewards greater.

The Law of Faith

As you learn to elevate your mind, you will learn to act more and more in faith. Faith is the key to unlocking the vault of God's economy. Faith runs ahead in Time and sees what your eye cannot see.

That is extraordinary! It means that when you act in faith and state "I Am," your faith moves forward in Time to perceive the good that is already waiting for you and begins reeling it in so it will manifest in your future. You must cast your faith outward, ahead of you into the future, and through focus and work and persistence, reel that destiny in.

Faith is the outline of what you desire. You just have to fill in the blanks. Life is not multiple choice! It is fill in the blank. How will you fill in the blanks? Life is like a coloring book—you choose the colors, God determines the lines. We all choose the life, adventure, situation we want. God has already chosen the destination. The question is, will you get there, and by what route? What colors will you choose, and will you stay inside the lines? This is the Law of Faith:

FAITH IS NOT AN ILLUSION. FAITH IS SUBSTANCE. YOUR FAITH IS ACTUALLY THE THING YOU WANT!

The actual manifestation is just a reflection of your faith. Faith is all that is real. Faith is required to please God, and without pleasing God nothing you have is possible. Just as when you touch something you are feeling atoms and the electrical charges between electrons, when you are experiencing something, it is faith you are experiencing. The thought and faith that produced the drama of your life are all that is real. Everything else is illusion, a result and reflection of faith.

Your thoughts are held prisoner in your mind waiting for a prison break. Think from the realm of your desire. What are you thinking from? From what direction are your thoughts coming—a place of faith or a place of doubt? When you think from faith, you break your thoughts free of their prison.

Send Your Thoughts Forth Like Messengers

There is a reality to match your legitimate longing, waiting for you in the cosmos. You are responsible for what shows up in your life, so you must acknowledge that whatever shows up was a legitimate longing in your mind, good or bad. Creative motives are power sources for influencing your thoughts—wealth, purpose, service, influence, home, family, love.

Your thought current must be sent in the direction of your life purpose. The current must be strong and running in one direction, and then thoughts that are unwelcome will be unable to penetrate. Think of your thoughts as a river, flowing toward the wealth, prosperity and opportunity that you desire. If the current of that river is weak or hesitant—if your thoughts are plagued with fear, doubt or distraction—then tributaries from other rivers will more easily be able to flow into your current and turn it aside. You might end up lost in a swamp of resentment and self-deception.

But if your current is deep, powerful and constant, then no other stream will affect it. Tributaries that flow into it will be consumed by the current and you will continue on to your destination: the ocean of Spirit and creative energy that is God.

You must be able to send your thoughts forth at all times as messengers of your intentions and your realization that you are *entitled* to the things you want to manifest. They are your property! There is a bad kind of entitlement, the idea that someone else owes you something that you did not earn. But the good kind of entitlement means you are worthy of something, you are confident that it is yours, and you know it is inevitable. You have already become the thing and taken title, and manifestation is just a matter of patience.

Single-Minded Purpose

When you have this kind of confidence and purpose, people who might bring bad things into your life are automatically excluded from your life. Your thoughts become bouncers at the door of your life. You can only connect with people with whom you resonate. All things resonate on a certain level of vibration—the chair you are sitting on, the food on your plate. Everything vibrates at a spiritual frequency, and like attracts like. Your vibration will attract those of a similar mind and repel those of the opposite mind, like a magnet attracts certain particles and repels others.

This is science, but it's also God. Remember this:

SCIENCE IS NOT AGAINST GOD; SCIENCE IS GOD.

The word science comes from the Latin root for knowledge, and what is God if not the root of all knowledge? God is omniscient, that is "omni-science." There is a science to creating the effects of your desire. That is why we are discussing these Laws.

You must always move toward thought concentration. You must live in the conviction that you are eternally progressing toward something higher in every atom of your being. Your faith resides in every atom—faith is the energy between subatomic particles. You must always proceed with that single purpose: to move your mind upward toward something greater, something more sublime, something grander and more giving.

As long as you have that singularity of purpose, you cannot be defeated. Remember the Tower of Babel? God favored the people as long as they maintained a single purpose to struggle upward. Once they disintegrated into fragmentation and bickering, God caused their ambitions to become curses. Distraction leads to fragmentation and failure.

Remember, the body has to be taught failure. That's why children don't know that things are impossible. They know no limits. Spirit has no limits, which is what we must re-learn as adults. The power of single-minded purpose and focused imagination is everything. If you move into unity in your thoughts, nothing can stop the outcome.

Keep the Group Moving Upward

Be sure that groups of people that you work with all share the same unity of thought and purpose; if one or two do not, they can bring down your entire endeavor. That is why just a few naysayers can destroy a startup company. Doubt is infectious, and human minds are heavy; they tend to sink with the gravity of doubt, rather than rise toward Heaven. You must always work hard to keep all minds in a group on an upward path.

This dynamic is why some groups take a while to start manifesting positive results. It is why some churches struggle to hit their stride and become prosperous; because too many of their members think that coming on Sunday is enough. It isn't. Any group must work wisely and effectively in the realm of thought and passion and focus if it is to create greatness.

* * *

SUMMARY

- Ask and it shall be given to you.

- You must train your mind to manifest good automatically.

- Passivity is a sin.

- Exaggeration, minimization, infatuation and resentment are the greatest lies.

- Each lie breeds seven more.

- Lies create an alternate reality of misfortune.

- Success has a look.

- The faith is the thing you want; all else is the reflection of faith.

- Science is God.

- Your thoughts must always be moving upward.

Chapter 16

THE LAW OF PLANNING

A ll things begin as air castles. Everything you will ever know or have begins as a creation of your imagination. Can you even conceive of something being able to come into being without existing in a mind first? Books, buildings, businesses, gourmet meals—everything had to be imagined and envisioned before it could manifest in physical reality. You first build your castle in your consciousness before you ever lay a foundation.

Your ability to envision is the key to manifestation. You must picture your desire in detail; if you picture the general, you will have little control over the outcome. You must be able to picture the specifics of what you want: what, where, how much, what kind. If you envision "a house," who knows what kind of house God will manifest in your experience? It could be a place worse than where you live now. You must "see" every aspect of your house in your mind's eye—the crown molding, the landscaping, the plasma television—everything. When you envision it, you are basically placing an order with the Universe's fulfillment house.

Wait, you say. Aren't I already a human being? That depends. Are you trying to make things manifest in your life by going after the material, by building with your hands? Then you're a "human doer." The currency of God's cosmic economy is not labor, but "I Am"—being the things you want and knowing that you are worthy of them. We have talked about how you must be the things you expect to manifest in corporeal reality. Well, you must be a "human being", envisioning yourself *being* the thing you want to have. Then doing becomes easy.

Your "Synchrodestiny"

You have the power to control your destiny. More than that—you are your destiny! There is no difference between what you will have and who you are becoming; they are the same thing. Part of your divinity is the ability to single-mindedly focus your attention on the desire you want in the future and bring it into manifestation.

That is "synchrodestiny," a state where you and your destiny are in synch. You are, therefore it is. This occurs when your awareness of who you are is perfectly in line with the things that are waiting to manifest for you. When you are completely the house, the car, the business, then you are in synchrodestiny. This is a sublime state that many people are never able to achieve, but you have the power to do so, because you understand the system and the secrets of manifestation.

In effect, God has shared with you one of His most astonishing traits: the ability to incarnate as many different things. Mythological characters have the ability to move from one incarnation to another. God wants you to do that. He wants you to incarnate into another being by changing the thoughts of what you want to become. You are your thoughts, and each time you change your thoughts, you re-vector—that is, you send on a new linear path—who and what you are becoming. You change the configuration of your air castle each time your thoughts take on a new incarnation.

All of us are living at the address of our thoughts. That is why it is so critical to maintain a singular focus of thinking. We never know when a stray thought will send our destiny moving in an unwanted direction. Every building was an air castle first. Everything begins with an idea. Ideas are part of the chemical formula:

~

IDEAS + FAITH + SINGULAR FOCUS = DESTINY

~

Each one of those things by itself has little power. Combine them and they are like the hypergolic fuel used to power space vehicles: a chemical reaction produces limitless energy that manifests as change.

Earth Is Canvas, Paint, and Brush

When you master these methods of thinking, earth becomes your canvas. For all of us, earth is neutral ground, ready for us to make it whatever we want it to be. For some people, it's hell, and others heaven, because of what they dream.

You are the sum total of what you create, no more and no less. What your thoughts give out, reality will give back to you. You get what you dream about, what you imagine and think. All men who have achieved great things have been dreamers. They were able to look beyond what *was* at the time they lived and see what was *possible.* By dreaming large and cultivating an unflagging vision of what could be done, they set an inevitable series of events in motion that ended in the airplane, the electric light, the computer, penicillin, and a thousand other earth-changing innovations. No one thought these things could exist before; no one even contemplated the possibility that reality could be bent so such things could exist. But the dream pressed them out into reality.

Stimulate Your Ambition

Your ambition should become your creed. Your single-minded vision to create what you know is possible must become the defining force in your life. Wake up the sleeping vibration that is your ambition by saying "I Am" the thing you wish to achieve, then focus on it with an unstinting, single-minded fury of creation.

Do not let other visions clutter the vision that comes to you from God.

You are kind of like Dr. Victor Frankenstein in Mary Shelley's famous novel. The body of what you want to create is ready and waiting on the table. All you need to do is breathe life into it. But tenacity is required. Do not let other visions clutter the vision that comes to you from God. If it is Godly, it will wait for you. Go after what is most important, and what is central to your vision. All things will happen in their time. This does have a wonderful side effect: working on one vision will often create effects that bring the other visions into reality as well. When you become a merchant of visions, your spiritual vibrations will create an effect that brings other visions into manifestation, even if you are not focused on them. You may even begin manifesting things for other people in your sphere!

Read books, learn and find out what you must do to stimulate your ambition. Know people who have done what you are trying to do. Expand your mind. Expand your relationships. Know people who are at the destination where you are trying to get. They can give you a map. That is why successful people consort with other successful people. The vibrations of success elevate everyone.

Dreams are a divine gift, intended to give you a glimpse of what is in store and to lift you out of the common into the uncommon—to show you what is possible! Pay attention to those dreams, for they are maps that can lead you to new destinies.

Do You Come to Church for the Wrong Reasons?

Church is a very misunderstood place. I think that in many cases, the word can be rearranged, a "t" added and an "h" taken away, and turned into "crutch." That's what church is for many Christians, even the saved. We come to church to escape Hell, to pray, to feel good about ourselves—all the wrong reasons.

There is only one valid reason to come to church: to develop insight into God's system and discover God's purpose for you. If you are coming to church because you feel that all God needs to give you is what you want, ask yourself:

"WHY THEN DO I NOT HAVE WHAT I WANT?"

The answer is simple: church is not what it's about! It's wonderful that you can come, be part of the community and hopefully give in a manner that supports prophecy, but until you can give in a way that supports the vision that you know you will manifest, church is little more than a self-esteem exercise. You should be able to walk away from church and walk into your true purpose in Spirit. What you walk away from determines what you walk into. Walk away until someone offers you not what you want, but what you *are*!

The Law of Planning

You cannot do all this randomly, you know. Try and you will fail. Mastering the Laws of Thinking is a complex, lifelong effort. More than that, you're going to be trying to maintain a purposeful focus of thought and attention on what you want, all while meeting people, carrying out tasks and creating. You cannot do all this without a plan. That is the Law of Planning:

~

IF YOU DO NOT HAVE A PLAN TO CREATE YOUR GOALS, YOU WILL FAIL.

~

People don't plan to fail, but they do fail to plan. In this complex world, you cannot maintain your focused, singular vision, and create what you want without a plan of action that guides the events of your day, sets out your goals, and defines the steps you need to take on the road to your destiny. It's simply too great a burden for anyone to bear without a map.

Keep a journal. Write down what you are supposed to do in your day. Do not approach your day and your life by just turning things over to God. God is not responsible for your life's path. It's up to you. If you don't map out your purpose, you will not get to your destination. There is a reason the words "destiny" and "destination" are so closely related.

What are you waiting for that is not happening right now? Chances are it's not happening because you do not have a plan to bring it into reality in your experience. Things will not just happen for you; you must make them happen with your attention and your declaration of "I Am." Something to remember:

REALITY CONTINUES WHETHER OTHERS ARE MAKING DECISIONS IN YOUR FAVOR OR NOT.

No one is obligated to bring something into manifestation for you; you must attract the manifestation with your thoughts and your energy. That is what a plan does: focuses the energy of your attention and your intention and strengthens it, even as a lens focuses the energy of the sun. Make a plan for creating your destiny that includes:

- Your actions each day.
- The types of people you want to attract.
- Your long-term goals.
- The thoughts you will focus on.
- A schedule for meditating and listening to God.
- A journal of your actions, thoughts and feelings.

Such a plan will be your blueprint for doing extraordinary things.

Provoke Action

You must create with Spirit. Only Spirit can create something that is everlasting and life-giving. The sweat of your brow cannot do this. Spirit does not need you to help it out. Spirit can do it itself. If you try to produce with anything other than Spirit, you will produce an Ishmael—a creature only of spirit.

Let blessings come and gobble you up. Let God overtake you. Give your money to God and watch it multiply. That is mastery! The Spirit will overtake you. It's like a corporate takeover from the CEO of the Universe! So provoke action—act and let things happen as they will. If you stay focused, the outcome will be what you want. Provoke action, get out of your comfort zone, and make things happen. You cannot go wrong when you do it with God in mind.

Today Is a Gift

All this is to say, live in this moment and let the next moment take care of itself. When we live in the future or the past, we are living in doubt and fear. Either we are regretting something in the past that we cannot change, or we are worrying about something in the future that our worry is going to bring about. Remember, you are a self-fulfilling prophet!

Live in today and you can live in joy and make the future what you envision. Stop looking for what's next. Turn yourself over to God's purpose and live in Spirit. You are here to enjoy life; that is life's purpose. When you do what gives you joy, you are fulfilling God's vision for you! Live in joy and you are closer to God. Savor the moments of your life. Know this and remember it:

THE PAST IS A THIEF. THE FUTURE IS UNKNOWN. TODAY IS A GIFT—THAT'S WHY THEY CALL IT "THE PRESENT."

Want is a thief, because want focuses on the future and what you do not have. Only the imagination matters, because it is creating your world in the present, every moment. Live in joy in the present, and trust that the path has set you on will prove right. Banish worry and love the day you are living in. Stop worrying and trying to control things—let the God in you create and inspire.

> *Only the imagination matters, because it is creating your world in the present, every moment.*
>
> ∼

Think about this: your world is creating itself every second. If your perceptions shape reality, then you are creating the future every moment, and everything you think and do shapes how it plays out. Nothing is set in stone; you are bound to nothing except God. You are free to create the reality you desire! It is rolling out in front of you like a carpet! Walk that path and don't worry about the floor. The floor is there and eventually, with focus, you will end up where you are meant to go. That is the greatest gift, other than His son, that God has given us all.

Leave the Past Behind

If you are creating the future in your mind with every moment, then you can see why it is so crucial to leave the past behind. You cannot change pain or guilt from your past; you can let it pollute the world you are unfurling in front of you right now, like a crack running through an otherwise sound piece of wood. If you let the crack become too large, it will splinter your material and what you are trying to build will not last.

Buddhists say the end of all suffering is acceptance. You suffer because you don't accept the moment, you don't accept the suffering of the past and let it go. When you dwell on it, you give it power over you. When you banish it, you make it powerless. Want equals suffering. Accept what's happening to you now. Leave the memories of the past and the wants of the future behind.

That is why I do not believe in therapy. The therapist violates your mind by making you relive the pain of years or decades ago—it cannot be coincidence that the word "therapist" breaks down thusly:

∼

THERAPIST = "THE RAPIST"

∼

Memories of anguish cannot benefit you; they can only harm you by making you doubt and fear. Accept what has happened, because you can't change it. Declare who and what you are and ignore the opinions of therapists or well-meaning others. Do not let yourself be defined by others.

The Blame Game

There's plenty of blame to go around, it seems. Everybody's got a finger to point at someone else—the government, Osama bin Laden, their spouse, God—for why things are the way they are. Why can't I buy a house? My boss. Why can't I get rich? My father didn't love me. The blame game is more popular than baseball. It's the national sport.

It's all nonsense. If you are responsible for what you call yourself and for the thoughts that you hold onto, then you are responsible for creating the future that unfurls in front of you. Blame is worthless. Point one finger and you'll find five fingers pointing back at you. No one can make you fear your past. No one can make you give what others think of you more weight than what you think of yourself. No one can make you refuse to listen to what God has to say. Everything is available to you, if you choose to take it.

The Laws of Thinking are the ultimate personal responsibility test. To master them, you must *know* that you are co-creator with God and that your choice is the ultimate power to create your reality. You came here to create and manifest—to have joy in why God has called you here. As long as you blame others, you will keep making the same mistakes. You cannot run away from yourself. As a wise man once said,

～

WHEREVER YOU GO, THERE YOU ARE.

～

* * *

SUMMARY

- You must be a human being, not a human doer.

- Synchrodestiny is when your destiny is in synch with your mind.

- Ideas + Faith + Singular Focus = Destiny

- The earth is neutral and will manifest whatever you call forth.

- You must stimulate your destiny with action.

- People often come to church for the wrong reasons.

- You need a plan.

- Reality keeps going no matter what you do.

- Your intentions create your future like a carpet unrolling in front of you.

- Let go of your past pain and fear.

Chapter 17

THE LAW OF MONEY

———•◦•———

The eye is the light of the body, and you are a law unto your-self. God does not direct your behavior; that is your decision. When you focus on what is wrong, you override the light of your convictions and you will pursue any behavior. When you override the light of your eye, then you override those convictions and you will do anything. You will get hooked on darkness. That is how people end up walking paths down to drugs, crime and self-degradation. The worst crime you can commit is self-destruction, because you have a choice and you choose to destroy God's potential in you. Therefore, walk in the light of your convictions. You are your own law, but you must deal with the consequences.

The Law of Money

Money is not the root of all evil. That's a mistake many peo-ple make. It says in the Bible that the *love* of money is the root of all evil. Money itself is a tool; it is the power of God made mani-fest in this world. Money is the power to effect change, to create and build. It cannot be evil; only what is done with it can be right or wrong.

Money is a force equal to God. Does that sound like blasphemy? It isn't—even the Bible says it. Scripture says, "You cannot serve God and Mammon." Mammon (the personification of money) is given standing equal to God. Money is god made manifest on the physical plane, but it is god without motive and will. God needs you to use money and apply your vision and "I Am" to make money do His will. But as you do that, as you use money to create and change and help others, you must take great care not to let money take the place of God. This is the Law of Money:

⌒

MONEY IS GOD'S POWER OF CHANGE IN THE WORLD.

⌒

You must conquer your love of money to conquer the evil in your life. If you want to do something, if you believe it is from God, then do it. The money will come. If you don't do something because the money not there, then you're listening to the money, not God. When you are working at one with God, you will act and create and spend money you don't have, *knowing* that God will provide. Remember, God likes it when you are out on the edge, stretching and taking risks and provoking with your actions. Act and the money follows.

Whose Voice Is Louder?

Does money have a louder voice than God? If you walk with God and faith, money does not have a hold on you. Which are you listening to, God or money? If you are acting without worry about money being there, then you are listening to God, and you'll always find money showing up in your bank account—in greater sum than it was when you emptied the account. When you sow in God, you reap more.

But when you act based on limits—when you say, "I can't do that" because the money is not in your hands—you are listening to money first. You are doubting God, and He will cast down what you are doing. God will always challenge you to do something that you cannot afford to do, challenge you to take those miraculous steps of faith out on the water and then turn and see the results. He will demand that you spend money you don't have in order to realize wealth beyond your dreams. The question is, will you do it? Your only money should be daily bread!

> *God will always challenge you to do something that you cannot afford to do . . .*

Know What to Do with Money

If you don't know what to do with money, money will not find you. Money must always be moving. The natural world, your breath, all is always moving! The only thing that should be still is your consciousness that you are god. But money should always be looking forward to giving, seeding and harvest.

God gives you a seed—your ideas, your creativity, your money. Everything exists within that seed. But you must release the seed for it to grow! If you do not, you have just signed up for lack. Everything you want exists already in seed form. Everything lies in seed time and harvest. Money is for sowing. If you do not sow, you will not harvest. You must get money moving, giving to others and creating, for it to grow and come back to you in greater abundance.

The world is full of people who fail to sow their seed because they spent it on their short-term needs. Do you know how many people have their house in their bellies? They ate their seed when their seed was for sowing. Instead of having faith and spending God's capital to create the house by giving or entrepreneurship, they spent the money in their hands and wasted it. When you don't sow your seed, you dishonor yourself. You dishonor the Lord.

You cannot honor God without capital. Capital is creation, and it is meant to be spread around. Give and use your money to create. Honor your father and mother; give them money to have long days.

Everything Begins with a Structure of Information

Everything you want to build must be purchased with the money of faith, and everything must begin as a mental structure before it can ever become a physical structure. Your new deck or your new home is an idea. The contractor merely places wood, stones and brick around the idea. The same is true of people. Everyone in your life shows up around the seed of your idea.

Everything else is raw material that your mind is attracting to it. Everything that comes at you first existed in you. Think about that: that means the negative in your life existed in you before it came along. So did the positive. These are the physics of mind—action, then reaction.

You must have the right information for your mind to produce the results that increase your favor and your prosperity. Your mind is a machine for manifesting that which God has ordained; information is the fuel that machine runs on. Bad information will produce bad results. When bad information gets passed on, look at the mind that is giving out the information. The mind shapes the information. Who are you listening to? That's why you have to watch new people; they might make changes to your system that will damage it. Study the habits of the rich. When you act without knowledge, there is a price to be paid.

Build It in Your Mind

We've talked about being specific when you create the vision for what you want. I suggest you write it down. Write out everything about what you will manifest in the next year, two years or five years. Write out how you will manifest, the process you will follow. Write out the results that manifestation will produce in your life. Then follow that blueprint to the letter.

In real estate, you have to follow the plans to the letter. If you deviate, you will create Hell on paper. If you build a house counter to the local planning regulations, you might find out that there's ground water where you didn't realize or something else you couldn't have known about. Set your own rules—then follow them! There are no short cuts. Everything we do in life must be preceded by a plan. Even children are born following a "birth plan" that details what the mother wants to have happen when she gets to the hospital.

The man who expects prosperity is constantly building his financial structure mentally. That's "Brain Building." What are you building in your mind? There must be the mental picture of success first; then building the structure is relatively easy. Seek the Kingdom of God first through your eye gate. Remember:

~

YOU MUST PERCEIVE IT AND CONCEIVE IT
BEFORE YOU CAN RECEIVE IT.

~

You Should Never Reach an End

The beauty of the Laws of Thinking and the economy of God is that the journey need never stop. Because there is no limit to what your mind can imagine, there is no limit to what God will manifest through Spirit in your life. But it is important that you keep a "never reach the end" mindset if you are to realize the glories in store.

The world's most successful individuals never reach a stopping point. For them, creation is both journey and destination.

The world's most successful individuals never reach a stopping point.

～

They know that to say, "I'm here, now I'm going to stop," is suicide for mind and Spirit. To be human is to keep striving and building and finding new challenges. If your goal is to keep giving, you will keep going. You must always have "further vision."

When you have a mentality that things "end," everything will be destroyed. You must always have a vision beyond your arrival point. If you do not, you will die—not physically, but in Spirit. Without a vision, people perish. You should always be moving forward in your mind and your vision toward something new.

This doesn't mean that you must always be working, or that you can't take a break if you've just spent years building a business. Don't forget, the purpose of this life is to have joy in it. You don't need to be working 24/7 to manifest God's intention; you just need to always be in an "I Am" mindset. Staying in that mental state frees you from work; when you live in that mental place, you can be on the beach in Maui and your Spirit will still be working for you. Inspiration is what brings things into physical reality, not perspiration.

Never Arrive

If you want to be truly happy, never develop an "arrival mentality." Never arrive. If you are worried about arriving, you have a material mentality, not a spiritual mentality. If you have a mind that says, "Okay, I reached that goal, but there are two new ones!" you will never lack for passion or joy. You will be like a traveler who gets up each morning excited about what the day's road will bring. The journey will be your joy.

The prize you earn when you work in God is your ability to keep going and chasing new goals—to keep reinventing your purpose. There can be no end, because if there is an end, there is no God. Endless movement forward is eternal purpose. Eternal purpose is eternal life.

Learn to Give

We come into the world selfish, and we must learn to be unselfish. Children come into the world selfish; they only know their own needs. Your job is to grow beyond childhood and remove the selfishness from your spirit. If you cannot do that, you are still a child, left behind in a world of adults who are growing and moving forward.

You must learn to do things you don't want to do—you must learn to give, not receive. You must master this truth:

~

RECEIVING IS THE REWARD FOR GIVING.

~

When you can give unselfishly without thought of reward, you are closer to your divine role as god than at any other time. Because giving selflessly is the act of sowing for another—of creating the potential and reality of good for another person, a community, or a company. When you give, you are truly with God.

Screaming children are a product of parents who have not gotten past their own selfishness. Women are always giving. They give blood every month; they give breast milk to their babies. That's why they live longer than men. Giving is the purpose of life. Giving is what sustains life!

* * *

SUMMARY

- Money is equal with God.

- Money is the power of change.

- Money is meant to be sown and moving.

- You must build it in your mind before it becomes a physical structure.

- You should develop a "never arrive" mentality.

- Receiving is the reward for giving.

THE LAW OF SYSTEM

———

As we enter the final three chapters of *The Laws of Thinking*, we're going to look at the most important aspect of using your mind to manifest the wealth and abundance that is your birthright: understanding God's *system*. We are frequently pursuing what we think is God, when what we really should be doing is working to understand His system. God works according to a system built on the Laws of Thinking, to create everything in the lives of every human being.

For example, one tenet of God's system is that He expects you to take action when there is no visible means of support. There are things God will tell you to produce when you think you have no visible means. Mary said, "I know not a man" when Gabriel came to her and revealed that she would bear Jesus. But the seed was within her. God wants you to see the Invisible Man within you, and stop looking without. Put yourself in at atmosphere of success, where the thoughts of people are real things and will guide your movement into the future.

Vision Sends You Provision

In order to become the successful thoughts that will bring you wealth, you need to have symmetrical clarity of thought—a simultaneous awareness of purpose and vision. Purpose gives you the power to anticipate the fulfillment of your vision and gives you an endless goal—not a single thing you must achieve, but a state of being that you will aim for all your life. In this way, the attitude that will bring your vision to life will become not an action, but a part of you. You become your vision, and when you do, you will never worry about stray thoughts damaging it.

You should always be chasing after a new vision. Your vision will keep sending you *provision*. That vision is what calls to money. Money does not lie there waiting for you; it won't come until the vision calls it. If you wait for money, you will never get started. You must be driven by your vision and not worry about the money. You must want the things and move toward it without the money. Money should never dictate what you can and cannot do. If it does, you are not trusting God.

God rewards those willing to take the leap onto the waters without knowing if they will be able to walk upon them. When you limit yourself by the money in your wallet, you will never have more then the money in your wallet! But when you create without worrying about how you will pay for it or tithe to the church even though you need that money to pay your electric bill, God will bring far more abundance back into your hands. It is the vision and acting upon that vision that buys what you want. Money is merely an effect of the real cosmic currency!

You must honor God with your substance, with the fruits of your work. Bringing an offering to the prophet means two things: you have discerned the prophet as the embodiment of God, and you are honoring God. When you give, you plant a seed. And the giving always seems like a bad deal if you are thinking only of what you are giving up, not that you are making a deposit in God's bank account. And when you do that, God will always pay you back with interest. God will repay your gift with His *interest* in manifesting what you desire!

Real Prophecy Brings Redemption

This is all wrapped up in the power and mysticism of prophecy. The prophetic word is your direct line to God. It is a translation of His Word into a seed of vision that lodges in your imagination and begins to grow. That seed, if planted and nurtured in proper season, will yield a glorious harvest. However, like with all other aspects of God's Laws, there are mazes and traps to beware of. Not all prophecy is created equal.

The prophetic word is your direct line to God.

Real prophecy is redemptive. It always comes with a solution. God will always speak with the answer to your situation in mind. Finding the answer is up to you; you will only find it if you are operating in awareness of Spirit. But God will never offer you a vision that does not include a blessing. Belief in the prophets and in redemption will allow you to recognize your answer from God when it comes in flesh form.

God embodies himself in the true prophet. Satan embodies himself in the prophet who comes to destroy your vision and pull your mind from the things you want. You must learn to discern the different voices and faces of God. You must recognize the man or vessel that God is moving through. If a prophet brings you a prophecy, and it has a redemptive aspect to it, then it comes from God.

~

GOD WILL NEVER SPEAK A PROPHETIC WORD TO YOU THAT DOES NOT COME WITH REDEMPTION.

~

If it does not, it is not from God.

Of course, it is up to you to *recognize* one kind of prophecy from another. One man might see a preacher ask for a tithe and think he is ripping people off. Others might see the same man and say, "No, he is setting them up for favor." To some, thunder is thunder. To others, it's God speaking. You must recognize what is what. If you can discern, you can get the blessing. You must hear the *theophonic* presence: the voice of God.

Don't Mistake Christianity for God

You must perceive God in His guises. Only then will you be free as Jesus made you. The Laws of Thinking are about altering your perceptions, the ultimate tools for altering your consciousness. You must learn to *discern*—to perceive with precision, see past illusions and instantly pick up the meanings of things.

For example, I go to yoga classes to improve my flexibility and my health. Now, ignorant or fearful people will say that when I go to yoga, I am worshipping the Hindu deities. That's wrong. That is not discernment. God is in everything in wholeness. People have said the devil was in everything: rap music, yoga, black people, Indians and much more. Don't mistake Christianity for God. They are NOT the same! God is all in all, and yoga is not a rejection of Him. Discern what is real and what is fear.

The opposite of discernment is demonization! In one, you recognize the embodiment of God in many things. In the other, you cannot discern, so you label instead. Discernment comes in wisdom, while demonization comes from ignorance and fear. Only in discernment can you perceive the wholeness of God. Only then can you see the Big Picture.

Each embodiment of God is a different part of that picture, a different part of the whole. Do not be put off when others do not believe what you believe. Because at the end of the day, Muslims, Jews, atheists, and everyone are just other faces of God—faces you have to love.

From the Church to the Kingdom

This is getting into the core of the economics of God. We spend so much of our time at church pursuing what we think God is, but what we're really doing is trying to have a relationship with the personality of God. We want to talk to God, be comforted by Him, and feel loved by Him, but we don't want to accept any of His demands. We would rather be passive and put all things in His hands. Well, let me tell you:

~

GOD IS NOT YOUR KEEPER.

~

Any more than your parent was your keeper or you are your child's keeper. You are a guide, a teacher, a mentor, and that is all. All else is passing on wisdom and lessons—your system for navigating life—to your children and letting them make their own way. In the same way, God does not want you to have an illusory relationship with Him; He wants you to move from the Church to the Kingdom. The Kingdom encompasses everyone of every faith.

213

THE LAWS OF THINKING

What is God's Kingdom? It is the system of Laws and modes of thinking that make possible the transition from Spirit to flesh, that allow God to express Himself in you. That Kingdom operates on vision; vision is birthed by memory and imagination and distorted by guilt. God will pull something from your memory to give you a vision of what can be, and that vision will be shaped by your imagination.

Fear and guilt paralyze your "imagination muscles." If you feel guilty about prosperity or opportunity, or fearful about failure, you will kill your vision. What are you afraid of? Fear of failure? Fear of success? Being part of God's Kingdom means forgetting about "having a relationship" with God and taking action. God is not looking for your adoration, but your action! Action is all. Take steps without fear, even if you don't know the outcome. Feel the fear, but do it anyway. Remember:

∼

MONEY ONLY SHOWS UP WHEN YOU HAVE VISION,
AND YOU CAN ONLY HAVE VISION WHEN
YOU ARE WITHOUT FEAR.

∼

Put Money in Its Proper Place

Earlier we said that money and God were equal. They are, but they are not separate. Money is god; it represents God's power working through you to change the world. Can you name a global-scale change that did not involve money? New medicines, new art forms, wars—they all require money. Those who say that money and God are somehow not related are either naïve or ignorant.

You cannot serve God and Mammon, but you must serve God *with* Mammon. Money must be put in its proper place to serve

God in order to manifest in your life. Money is not evil unto itself; it becomes sinful when you get out of balance and elevate it to a place above God. When you serve money instead of God, it will control your day. Only God can save you. Do not depend on money; depend on God. Give money to God and God will multiply your money and give it back to you in greater sum.

For example, if you live in a marvelous house and drive a spectacular car to work every day, you could easily become so enamored of these possessions that you let your fear of losing them drive your actions. You stop taking risks because you do not want to lose your house. But did not Jesus say that the man who tries to save his life will lose it? You must give; you must be willing to risk all, every day, with God as your currency. God is like the Cosmic Accountant; if you place your money with him to manage, He will multiply and bring it back to you in greater amount.

The Real Mark of the Beast

He also forced everyone, small and great, rich and poor, free and slave, to receive a mark on his right hand or on his forehead, so that no one could buy or sell unless he had the mark, which is the name of the beast or the number of his name. Here is wisdom. Let him that hath understanding count the number of the beast: for it is the number of a man; and his number is Six hundred threescore and six.

— Revelation 13:16-18

This passage from the book of Revelation has been the most misunderstood, misquoted source of more fear and stupidity than any other part of the Bible. People spend their time looking for the Beast, adding up the numbers of people's names, crazy stuff like

215

that. Do you want to know what the mark of the Beast really is? I'm going to tell you right now. You'll never look at the film "The Omen" the same way again.

In Revelation, the scripture says that we will find the mark in the hand or the forehead of those who have been marked. That means those people are marked in the consciousness of their hand and the consciousness of their mind. What is the 666? Man was created on the sixth day. The scripture makes the point that no man can buy or sell without the Mark. So:

THE MARK IS WHEN YOU ARE BUYING AND SELLING AS MAN, NOT AS GOD.

The Mark means you are doing what you can afford. You are allowing yourself to be limited by the money in your hand; then you are the Beast. You must spend without money! If you can do that, your money cannot dictate to you how you can do something. You should dictate to your money how something will be done!

People with the Mark of the Beast are limiting themselves with their concern over money. They are spending money as their currency. Money is their god and all they can perceive is the limited world defined by the money they hold in their hands. They have no vision and they perish! But people whose currency is the Name of the Father—these are people who are not limiting themselves. They are becoming what they want in their vision and making it manifest. They are spending God as currency.

God says, "Come buy without money." Buy with your divinity, not your humanity. When you get something because of your divinity, your "I Am" consciousness, your Godliness (god-like-ness), no one can take it away. If they do, you will produce another. The material ceases to be important to you, because you have an unlimited supply of abundance.

Don't care about what something costs! Be the thing you want.

But when you get something with the Mark of the Beast—when you have been limited by your salary—you will act like a beast when anyone threatens what you have. Because you appraise the thing above divinity. Don't care about what something costs! Be the thing you want. Every time you do something, you leave a Mark! Which Mark is it?

The Law of System

Don't ever let the price make the difference in what you can or cannot accomplish. You must learn to buy what you desire in your state of consciousness that "I Am that." When you start thinking, "I am that house," that house starts thinking it is you. The Beast is trying to get you to do things within your means. If you limit yourself that way, you will never follow your vision and imagination, because you will fear. You will never manifest what God has in mind for you.

You have to be willing to give away all you have in order to get more. Tithing is child's play. Any beast can tithe. The test is giving more to God than you give to the government. Giving money away is an act of trust in God; you are telling Him that He is your currency expressed in you as "I Am." God is your money; money is not your god!

Giving is an act of trying to bring something to you. People often think giving money to the prophet is an act of greed. Those who cannot see will tell you that the prophet is ripping you off for that which cannot be seen. But if that were the case, how do you explain the incredible blessings that have appeared in the lives of the people of my own church who have given without question? If you are firmly in the love of money, you will not perceive the invisible currency that is moving wheels and destiny in your life.

Seek the Kingdom—the system—of God. Everything in the Universe operates based on a system. Your body operates according to multiple systems—nervous, circulatory, digestive, and so on. Everything must work within the system for good to result. Take the solar system: move the sun one degree and you either burn or freeze. When you are sick, your body systems are not working. All systems must work harmoniously.

Witchcraft is rebellion. A witch is one who tries to cut across the system, to get something for nothing, ignoring the laws of cosmic economics. Romans 16:17 says, *"Now I beseech you, brethren, mark them which cause divisions and offences contrary to the doctrine which ye have learned; and avoid them."* Rebellion can bring down the system. When you are sick, one of those systems is out of order. It is saying, "I want to be rebellious." Tithing is a system, and if you do not tithe, you are rebellious.

This is the Law of System and it couldn't be simpler:

～

THE RICH ARE RICH BECAUSE THEY UNDERSTAND
AND OBEY GOD'S SYSTEM.

～

If you want to be wealthy, get into the principles and system of God rather than just the personality of God. *Money is waiting for an idea to emerge out of you so it can latch on.* Otherwise you will become one of those people who are saved, but who miss out on their prosperity.

Do Not Curse the Rich

The system of God is everything we have talked about so far in this book. Prosperity begins in the mind. Prosperity is already out there for you, already ordained. You must know the system that captures it, that creates "psychogenesis," a word that literally means "create with the mind." When God created the cosmos, that was psychogenesis. He created everything with a Word spoken from His mind.

You are only as rich as your mind can conceive and perceive. To find prosperity in your mind, your mind must be amenable to it, not hostile. You must love the rich. There's an unfortunate trend in this country today to revile the rich, as if being rich was by itself some kind of sin. I will be the first to admit that there are many rich people who love Mammon, not God, and who use their wealth not to help others but to elevate themselves. But most wealthy people are hardworking people who understand that when you are hostile to the rich, you have impoverished thoughts. You cannot curse the rich and be rich. Wealth is a tool; it's neutral. How you use it determines good or ill.

Your curse of the rich carries your voice to the Universe, telling it that you are not supposed to be rich. The rich are connected with rich ideas and thoughts. They spend their time with rich people, move enormous sums of money, drive rich cars and live in rich houses. They broadcast to the Universe, "This is what I am supposed to be! This is who I Am!"

Cast thy bread upon the water. Whatever you cast in the Kingdom you will find in many days. You will reap in due season if you stay the distance. Your harvest, your wealth, will come if you can be patient. Do not rush God. Trust Him and He will bring you all that you ask for.

Know Your Pattern

Another part of the system the rich follow is having a pattern. They know what they are after and go after it with the power of focused intention. It is fatal to work for one thing and expect something else. Everything must be created mentally first, then it follows that mental pattern.

Prosperity follows a pattern. The rich develop a pattern of thinking and acting in their lives that produces prosperity. You cannot become prosperous if you half-expect to remain poor. You must be fully persuaded and ask for what you know you already deserve. You cannot be at war with yourself and be prosperous. Prosperity wants to know if you live worthy of this state of con-sciousness. What is the way you live—telling prosperity that it should embrace you or pass you by?

Your thoughts shape the music of prosperity. Music follows a pattern, as you know: measures, beats, keys and a time signa-ture. But if the conductor and players do not follow the pattern the result is just ear-splitting noise. In the cosmic economy, God is the conductor and you are part of the orchestra. If you do not to shape the sound to what you want, you have a cacophony. If you have God's system in your mind, you will follow the pattern and you will achieve the music that you want.

Everyone has his signature pattern, his signature system. The rich do not leave their patterns, because they know the result will be disaster. You see, no one ever gets rich by accident. The wealthy have patterns of behavior and of thinking that create the results they seek and manifest wealth in their lives. Watch the patterns the rich follow and learn from them. In time, you will become aware of the pattern that works for you:

- The people you know.

- The goals you set.

- Your thoughts to start the day.

- Your tithing and giving habits.

- The way you explain setbacks.

Once you know your pattern, do not deviate from it. Everything in life has an arrangement. Jesus did not do anything he did not first see the Father do. You cannot live in hope; you must live in certainty. If you are working for one thing and expecting something else, you are a hypocrite. And you cannot live as a hypocrite.

> *Everything in life has an arrangement. Jesus did not do anything he did not first see the Father do.*

Reject the Rejectors

Watch out for people who come into your world and try to disrupt your pattern. You must know no defeat in your mind before you can achieve it. Nothing must disrupt your self-esteem. Success has a look, feel, stride, sound and smell. When you achieve success, that look, smell and feel will attract the naysayers as a horse attracts flies.

The naysayers serve the purpose of God. They are testing you to see if you are living worthy of the success you have manifested— to see if you will remain focused on God as the source or lose yourself to Mammon or to self-doubt. You must reach the level of mastery in life where you are proficient at rejecting rejection.

Learn to celebrate rejection. Rejection and disdain are your gauges of how worthy your idea is. The greater the rejection, the greater the anointing. Rejection is the crucible of how you believe in your idea. Can you believe it into being? Life does not celebrate sameness; it celebrates uniqueness. Life rewards originality. Artists, writers, musicians, directors, actors—the ones who demonstrate daring, brave originality are rewarded. From Bob Dylan to Kanye West, Pablo Picasso to director Spike Jonze, risk takers are celebrated. They pay no attention to rejection. They listen to the voice shouting inside their imaginations and act accordingly.

Become "Thinkful"

Tapping into God's system to create wealth is a matter of training your thoughts. You must refuse to consort with poverty. Poverty in Spirit will spread poverty. Think poor and you will become poor. You cannot be thankful until you are "thinkful."

Few people in this world will recognize the actions of someone working within God's system and thank them for the blessings that result. Perhaps ten percent of people, no more, will see what has been done and will thank someone for it. People who think understand not only what is valuable, but know why it has value! Try to have only thinking, thanking people in your life.

Right thoughts produce miracles; wrong thoughts generate disasters. You've got to train yourself to think progressively, creatively, constructively, inventively, abundantly and optimistically. Life only rewards creativity, risk and optimism.

What Direction Are You Facing?

Here's something to master and internalize:

YOU WILL GO IN THE DIRECTION THAT YOU FACE.

You will move according to the orientation of your mind. If your thoughts are oriented on success and on the creation of daring, brave, original things, then you will attract those things and people who think similar thoughts into your orbit. If, on the other hand, your mind is oriented on doubt, fear and envy, you will attract misfortune and want in your life, as well as people who will bring you low. You will go in the direction you are facing.

You can usually see where people are headed. If someone has successful ideas, mentors, friends and partners, it's obvious. It's equally apparent when someone has an orientation toward expecting disaster, because disaster always somehow seems to manifest. If all you see are problems in your life, then you are facing in the direction of problems. The tricky part is, you may not even be aware of a problem until someone else brings it to your attention. Having the wrong people in your life can *create* problems without you being aware of them until it's too late.

Then again, if you are facing in a direction of answers, you will create answers. Something free is worth what you pay for it. Do not look toward quantity, but quality. Quantity will break your back, but quality can build nations. You must build a system that will bring quality into your life. Quality people will become your allies, strategists, and the people who will change your life.

Mastering the system of God demands that you become your own disciple. Become a person of quality and advanced mind, a disciple of yourself as god, as "I Am." There will be no limit to what you can achieve.

* * *

SUMMARY

- Vision will send you provision.

- A prophecy that is from God will always have redemption in it.

- Learn to discern, not demonize.

- You must discover the Kingdom, not the personality of God.

- Money only shows up when vision calls to it.

- You cannot serve God and Mammon.

- The Mark of the Beast is when you buy and sell as man, limited by money.

- The rich understand God's system.

- Wealth follows a pattern.

- God favors the rejected, courageous, original thinker.

- You will go in the direction you face.

Chapter 19

THE LAW OF PROSPERITY

———•———

Let them shout for joy, and be glad, that favor my righteous cause: yea, let them say continually, Let the Lord be magnified, which hath pleasure in the prosperity of his servant.

— Psalm 35:27

If you aspire to be wealthy and to work within God's system, you must also understand the nature of prosperity. For some reason, a mythology has grown around God that insists He loves poverty; that only the poor are truly holy, and that to be one with God you have to give up all your worldly possessions and live in a cave. That is ridiculous! You are the utmost expression of God, pressed out from His Spirit into this material realm, so why would God want Himself to be poor? It doesn't make any sense.

In truth, God takes pleasure in your prosperity. He rejoices when your needs are met. It's like watching your kid hit a home run in Little League: God is there cheering for you to do great

225

things and be successful. When you achieve greatness, He does as well. Remember, God has no existence on this plane without you, so your riches also enrich God!

God is interested in your abundance. It is the will of God for you to become all things you are capable of becoming in the divine order. This is an inherent part of human nature. You are meant to be prosperous and wealthy, to prosper in all things. Where people make the mistake is this:

~

THEY ASSUME THAT TO HAVE WEALTH IS TO WORSHIP WEALTH.

~

This is a fallacy. Does it occur? Yes. There are men and women out there who have been seduced by the money in their bank accounts rather than the wealth of their "thanks account," the gratitude they owe to God for being the source of all their good fortune. But it is not inevitable that you become enamored of wealth and put it before God. The only people who have to do that are those who *lack the strength to be both wealthy and godly.* Well, I'm here to tell you that you can do both; you can have great material riches and not be captivated by them. You need not be one of the weak who thrust wealth away from themselves saying, "No, I can't handle the temptation!" You can handle the temptation! You can have gold, but let gold have no power over you. You can do what God has always intended: have wealth and use it to serve Him.

It Is Natural to Want More

It is in our divine natures to want more, to gravitate toward abundance. Becoming rich is Godly. The objective of life is development and growth, and the basis of all advancement must be the science of getting rich. That is what the Laws of Thinking are about! Wealth is not sinful; money is a tool, like anything else. Its sinfulness or saintliness lies in how you use it. That's all. Everything comes back to your choices. That is the inherent fear and wonder of God's system. If you have the courage to face your choices, you can be wealthy and yet wealth will never be your master.

We have an inborn, divine desire to manifest and create and grow and advance...

Every person naturally wants to be rich, to be and have all that he or she is capable of being and having. This is the way God designed us. We have an inborn, divine desire to manifest and create and grow and advance—to realize the possibilities inherent in our nature. Think about it—in just 100 years we have gone from traveling around filthy, disease-ridden cities in horse-drawn wagons to hopping continents in supersonic jets, unlocking the human genetic code, and creating the Internet, the most powerful communication tool ever devised, just for starters! Our natural state is to advance, to make use of things. And you can only have use of things if you become rich enough to buy them.

It is the will of God for you to have rich ideas and the means to bring those ideas into physical reality. It is normal and right to want to become rich. To put this another way:

IT IS ABNORMAL NOT TO WANT TO LIVE ABUNDANTLY.

Abundance is your right. It is the will of God that you have enough money to buy the things you want.

The Law of Prosperity

You need to start getting rid of your poverty consciousness if you're going to attract the wealth that God has ordained for you. God has His life through you, so if you don't allow yourself to be prosperous, you constrict the life of God. That is an offense to God. God wants you to declare that you deserve everything; it is not His will for you to live in want. To be content with less is sinful—it stunts the potential God has placed in you. It limits God!

But prosperity means more than simply having material wealth. What good would it be to have millions of dollars and be bedridden? Or to have your days crippled by worry? Prosperity also means health and peace of mind. It means that you are whole. It is God's will for you to walk in wholeness. You need to reach out for more than just money, but wholeness! When you live as a whole person, balancing the three properties that God desires for you, then you are carrying out His intention to its fullest. That is the Law of Prosperity:

∼

WEALTH + HEALTH + PEACE OF MIND = PROSPERITY

∼

We live for three motives at the same time: the body, the soul and the mind. All three must be served. None is better, holier or more desirable than the others, and none can fully live or serve God without the others. You can have a soaring soul and visions of greatness, but if you do not take care of your health, your body will not allow you to do everything you need to make your vision manifest.

And if your body is sound but your mind is slack and slow because you have not educated yourself, you will lack the knowledge to do all you can to fulfill God's intention. All three aspects of the self must live fully if you are to express yourself and God fully.

No one believes that God is poor. God has all the riches of the Universe at His fingertips. When you live according to His system and pursue riches, a healthy body and the peace of mind that comes with serving your passion and caring for your fellow man, you become truly divine.

It Takes Faith to Be Rich

Everything begins in the mind and projects outward. There must be a crippling thought inside you before there can be a crippling effect outside of you. The external body is only as prosperous as the soul is. When you act in faith, you prosper. When you act in doubt, you will suffer.

It does not take faith to be poor; it takes faith to be rich. There is no pleasing God without faith. Poverty doesn't need faith, but prosperity does. It takes no faith to live paycheck to paycheck. Faith is when you move beyond the norm and trust God. Faith is when you say, "I will not be limited by my paycheck. I will see and do those things that have nothing to do with what I have and trust God to pay for them."

The power of faith to achieve wealth is virtually without limit, once you acknowledge that all wealth stems from opening your Spirit to rely on God, take risks and let Him create the resources needed to fill the void you have just jumped out into. Faith is an optimist; faith always sees a way out. Faith sees a door when there is no door. Faith will never let you fall when you jump; it will always reach out to God and produce a parachute made of $100 bills!

Doubt is the opposite of faith. Doubt can't see a door even when there is one. Doubt is a pessimist. Are people in your life feeding your faith or your doubt? Faith moves mountains, while doubt piles fears on top of one another. You must feed your faith and starve your fears. Faith opens the door of ability and develops superiority. You start to transcend your own limitations. When you take a risk without fear and realize two things—that God does indeed provide for your safe landing and that you have the innate ability to persevere through uncertainty—what will you do? You will take more, greater risks and do greater things!

The Rich "Think Differently"

I laugh when I hear people say that the rich are no different from anyone else. You ever notice that it's poor people who say that? Let me tell you the hard truth:

THE RICH THINK DIFFERENTLY FROM THE POOR.

The rich are different. That's how they became rich! They don't acknowledge limitations. The rich live in uncertainty and take risks, because they have faith in their ability to overcome uncertainty. They act on faith, not fear. Fear does not stop them. The rich don't want; they know *they* are the key to unlock what they want. How would Richard Branson or Oprah Winfrey have been able to build their empires if, every time someone told them, "You can't do that, it's a crazy idea," they had said, "Maybe he's right. Maybe I can't do that"? Instead, they act without fear, because they have internalized the idea that if they jump and take the risk, good things will happen.

People who are successful know, with the same certainty that you know the sun will rise in the morning, that if they make the leap of faith, no matter what happens they will somehow land okay and make the best of whatever occurs. And let me tell you, God shows *great* favor to those who do that!

We must *expect* greatness from ourselves. You cannot succeed with an attitude of weakness, doubt and fear. Conquer with your eye first, then conquer with your hand. Faith annihilates obstacles and moves mountains. Abraham, Joshua, Moses and others were able to perform miracles through faith. Without it you can do nothing. A strong man loses power when he loses confidence in his ability to act in faith. You must train yourself to have no doubt in your ability to create the best outcomes—you must always act like a winner and emit winning ideas!

> *You cannot succeed with an attitude of weakness, doubt and fear.*

Unexpressed Desire Becomes Disease

You are God expressed into this world; you are God's energy and thought playing out on the material plane. Your purpose is to express your desires and fulfill God's purpose. That is your highest, best calling. When you attend to your desires and do everything you can to fulfill them, you are living and moving in Spirit, one with God. When you do not, you open yourself to sickness. Know this, then:

WHEREVER THERE IS UNEXPRESSED POSSIBILITY OR FUNCTION NOT PERFORMED, THERE IS UNSATISFIED DESIRE.

Desire is possibility seeking expression. Desire is function seeking performance. You are meant to fully express the possibility that lies within you. When you are not expressing what you desire, you are making yourself sick inwardly. Proverbs 13:12 says, *"Hope deferred maketh the heart sick: but when the desire cometh, it is a tree of life."* Desire is your tree of life. When you bottle up your desires, you bring stress into your life and you can force the systems of your body out of balance. That is the source of disease.

When you do not express your desires, you are in want. Expressing desire—pursuing and attaining the things you want—is your highest expression of yourself and of God's will. When you think about it, depression is a lack of expression. A woman who has post partum depression has expressed her child, the thing she had desired most. Now that the child is born, she is without purpose, at least in her own mind. She needs to find another way to express. It is this hunger for expression that is behind the "biological clock" ticking feeling that many women experience. Women and men are creators and *expressors*. It is as natural to us as breathing!

No One Is More Misunderstood Than God

The path of the Laws of Thinking is fraught with misunderstanding. There will always be people who, when you come into your own and create your prosperity, will not understand and will try to cast you down as a result. God knows; God is the most misunderstood of all beings. We attach so much baggage to His cart and we don't even see the beautiful simplicity of His system: if you give freely of yourself, your passion and your money without worrying about support, God will provide the support.

Others will frequently fail to understand this. The path others have for you will be different than what God has in mind for you. When you come boldly before the throne of God, you will get grace and favor unmerited, and other people will not understand why. They will see that they have done good works and do not receive the same favor, and that is because *favor is not fair*. Favor does not come as payment for good works; it comes when you follow God's system. It comes when you sow the seed of courage and vision and attention and create a harvest that fully expresses what is inside you, bursting to get out.

You must tithe and give, because the seed is what gives you grace. The seed is what makes you a co-heir with Jesus. The sown seed makes the angel act on your behalf. God wants you to prosper, but your prosperity is tied to how you obey the Word of God. You must provide for those of your house. You must honor your family with money, which is God made material. If you do not provide, you are an infidel. You are denying the system of God and denying faith.

You are thought. If your background thoughts are negative, they will eat away at your prosperity like termites. That is why it is so important to have a positive background soundtrack of thought, running through your mind at all times. If you can achieve that, you will never have to worry about the sabotage of negative thoughts. Your thoughts—even your dreams while you are asleep—will be *programmed* to manifest wealth and prosperity!

* * *

SUMMARY

- God wants you to be prosperous.

- Not wanting to live with abundance is abnormal.

- Wealth + Health + Peace of Mind = Prosperity

- It takes faith to be rich.

- The rich think differently from the poor.

- Unexpressed desire will make you sick.

- You will be misunderstood.

THE LAW OF THE HARVEST

———•———

Finally, we come to the end of our journey, but the beginning of yours. You have discovered much about how your thought ties in with the intention and expression of God, and you have begun to discover your own divine nature as "I Am" and to come into your power as god. Now, in this last chapter, it is time to look at the exact process by which your thoughts become things. When you fully understand this process, you will be ready to begin manifesting greater and greater things in your life.

The Process of Manifestation

1. You have a *thought*. To manifest, this thought must come to you from God, when your mind is at peace and you are open to listening to God's voice. Then His speech will take the form of thoughts that you know require expression.

2. You have a *feeling*. Your thought must spark an emotion in you; you must feel the desire to turn your thought into manifestation. Feeling clothes your thought. Emotion moves thought along; that's why it's called "e-motion."

3. You have a *vision*. Your imagination sees how that thought can become reality. Once you feel it, you can see it. Upon the vision entering your mind, you give the thought form and begin to manifest it in the Spirit realm, where it is waiting for you to attract it to you.

4. You set *goals*. Goals are the frame that the picture you see fits in. Goals make things more specific, so Spirit knows what to express. You cannot get anywhere unless you know where you are going.

5. You make *plans*. Plans are the steps you must take to move your goal from thought to physical experience. Plans tell you your direction and lend direction to your efforts.

6. You take *action*. Once you have goals and plans in place, you must walk the walk. All faith must have corresponding action. Faith without action is idleness, and it is an offense to God. If you procrastinate, you attract the thief of your vision. The only reason you don't have what you want is because you haven't taken action!

7. You see *results*. Results will always come in response to your action. Whatsoever you sow, so shall ye reap. You will always produce results; the type of results you produce will depend on how well you follow the steps. Just as important, whether or not you continue to manifest results depends on your persistence in following the steps again and again.

There it is: the secret to incarnation laid out for you. God used the exact same process to create the Universe: He had a thought, felt it was good, had a vision of Man and the earth, set goals, made His plan to have Man come forth and express God in the material realm, and took action with His Word. Following the seven steps makes you truly co-equal with God, because you share His methods.

⌇

YOU CANNOT SHARE SOMEONE'S METHOD OF DOING SOMETHING UNLESS YOU SHARE HIS STATURE.

⌇

If there is a failure in manifestation, it means you missed a step in this process. That means you must go back and check the process. Did you do it all right? Did you have the right vision? Did you set the right goals? Did you make a good plan? Did you take consistent action? This is how you move things from the unseen to the seen.

God Commands

God is in the business of commanding. He gives you instructions to help you when you are in a financial crisis, but make no mistake. This is not advice. This is a command. This is, "Do it this way, or the results will not be so hot." God will not make you do anything, but He will give you a command and let you know that doing things according to His system is definitely in your best interest.

Part of God's command to help you express your innermost desires will always be to do something that you are not prepared to do. God is a god of risk. He loves it when His children fully accept their roles as co-Creators and make the leap of faith into something that seems impossible. That is what God does. Think about it: at the Creation, there was no world for God to base his actions on. He didn't have a blueprint of success to work from. He took a risk and created the Seen from the Unseen. God *is* risk. Risk is what will bring you your harvest, and harvest is really what all this material is about! God will always command you to do something that you are not prepared to do, or to declare something that is out of character for you at the time.

Risk is what will bring you your harvest, and harvest is really what all this material is about!

~

God also commands you to give to Him out of the first fruits of your labor. Proverbs 3:9 says, *"Honor the Lord with thy substance, and with the first fruits of all thine increase."* Honoring the Lord means tithing, giving of your money to the prophet, giving money to your parents, honoring your father and mother with wealth. If you do this, you can rest when you don't see manifestation, because you know that when you honor the Lord by giving to Him, manifestation will come. But know this:

~

NOT ONLY IS FAVOR NOT FAIR, IT IS NOT FREE.

~

Favor comes with a price, and only those who are willing to pay the price—and use the right currency while doing it—will receive favor. Some people come to church every weekend and pray like there's no tomorrow, and give the minimum and wonder why they have not received God's favor. It's because you're trying to buy favor with the wrong currency! You can't buy something in New York with money from Saudi Arabia. You must use the money that works in the system in which you are working. You must purchase your favor with faith and by giving in a way that validates that faith—that shows you are not limited by money.

What Is Your Response?

Events happen in our lives, and we cannot usually control them. But what we can control is our *response* to the things that happen. Your response to something will always determine what you will receive from that thing. Sometimes, the manifestation you have been waiting for will hang on a thread, just barely unseen, waiting to see if you believe the Word more than what you see. The manifestation is waiting to see what your response will be!

~

WHEN YOU CHANGE YOUR RESPONSE,
YOU CHANGE THE OUTCOME.

~

That is why you cannot respond in fear to any event. Fear paralyzes. Fear generates its own outcomes. Every event deserves a response, but you can choose how to respond. You can choose what to name the people in your life. You can choose to look at the loss of a job as a disaster, a reason to mourn and panic and worry about money and stop giving. Or you can look at the same event as an opportunity to step outside your comfort zone and start the business that God has sown as a seed in your mind. Remember, God loves to spin you around and take away visible support from your life so that you are forced to turn in new directions.

How you respond will determine the results you produce. Your response is your harvest. The person who responds to a job loss with panic will rush out and take any job he can find. He will sell himself back in to slavery at the very moment when he had the chance to set himself free! The person who does not panic, who responds to this event as a turning point ordained to allow him to make a change, will get excited and start creating opportunity. God never panics. He simply responds. This is the Law of Harvest:

EVENT + RESPONSE = HARVEST

There are entrepreneurs out there who will tell you that even though their businesses are successful, the most energized they get is when they lose a big client and they are faced with the challenge of going out and finding new business! *That* is the response that makes greatness. What are you naming the circumstances and situations of your life? What you name them determines whether they are blessings or curses. Relax and name things in a way that makes them positive and makes them serve you. Your response will determine your miracle!

The Seasons of Your Life

> *To every thing there is a season, and a time to every purpose under the heaven.*
>
> — Ecclesiastes 3:1

The outcome of events is your harvest. What you sow with your giving, your faith, your actions and your response to events will be your harvest. These things always produce a harvest; the nature of the harvest will depend on how well you follow the rules God has set down.

Your life comes in seasons, seed time and harvest, just as the farms and fields of the world do. There are four seasons in our lives:

- **Spring**—the first 21 years of your life are your springtime. This is when you are being born and created. You are growing in body, mind and spirit and discovering your desires.

- **Summer**—from age 21 to 42, you are in your summertime. This is not a time for vacationing; only poor people vacation in summer. Summer is when you do your work, make your plans, and lay the foundation for your harvest.

- **Autumn**—from age 42 to 63, you are in autumn. This is the time for harvest. This is when everything you have done comes to fruition and you make your money. This is when you are raking in everything you planted in summer.

- **Winter**—from age 63 on, you are in winter. This is your time to rest and relax, to enjoy the harvest you spent so many years creating. You should not have to go out and work any longer. When a person retires and then has to go out and work after 63, they violated a previous season. They did not do what they were supposed to do in a previous season.

The seasons are a way of imposing order upon Time and upon human activity. Remember, before creation everything was without form and void until God gave it order. Even the Spirit has order. God always moves according to a plan.

Do You Have the Glory of God?

God commanded everything He created to multiply. God shows up in your life to create, multiply and cause something you already have to become more. That is the purpose of creation: to develop, multiply and expand. People and events that come from God are in your life to help you multiply your harvest and add to your wealth. Lack of productivity is an insult to God. God's curse will wither what you hope for.

Whenever a person shows up in your life who multiplies your blessings, that person is from God. It could be a business partner, a mentor, an investor or a creative thinker. If that person brings joy and new ideas into your world, and sparks you to take new risks, he or she is a blessing from the Lord. Someone sent by Satan will only create to divide and rob.

When you are working with people who help you multiply your wealth and increase your prosperity, you are working in God's glory. *Glory is wealth.* There is no other meaning that holds true to God's purpose. The meaning of glory is made clear in the first mention of the world in the Bible, when Laban complains that Jacob has taken all their father's livestock:

> *And he heard the words of Laban's sons, saying, Jacob hath taken away all that was our father's; and of that which was our father's hath he gotten all this glory.*
> — Genesis 31:1

According to *hermeneutics,* the science of interpreting Scripture, there is something called the Law of First Mention. A word's first mention will carry that meaning for the rest of the text. Under this interpretation:

242

~

GLORY = WEALTH.

~

Glory will always make you stronger. Glory increases itself. Giving glory to God means giving wealth to God through the prophet and creating wealth for God that empowers Him to effect change in this world through the power of money.

You will become wealthy by admitting God's presence into your life. His "presence" will produce His "presents." God's glory is wealth. That is the splendor of God, the excellence of His presence. That is the Kingdom. Wealth is God's glory in your life, and your wealth is glory in God's life.

People cannot always see this. Some people will not understand when you throw them something of value if they are not working in God's system. Not everyone can see. That's why people get upset with mentors; they do not perceive that when a mentor appears to be knocking them down, he's actually trying to help them rise higher.

Not everyone will see glory as glory or blessings as blessings. Their response is wrong. Some will think you're trying to rip them off when you're trying to make them rich. God is always moving through His people. The challenge is always on. God comes in many disguises. You must always be honing your perception and growing in wisdom and discernment.

Your Meditation Is Your Medication

The more you understand the intersection of mind and Spirit with the things we achieve in the material world, the clearer it should be that nothing happens at the level of the physical without happening in the unseen world first. For example, the body does not get sick. Only the mind gets sick. In Matthew 9:20, the Bible speaks of *"And, behold, a woman, which was diseased with an issue of blood twelve years, came behind him, and touched the hem of his garment."* The woman had issues! An issue of blood is an issue of family, some curse or grudge against a member of her family that she had been carrying around for twelve years. It took Jesus to make her aware of it and speak a different word to herself and be healed.

> *What you don't confront will settle on the inside of you and will manifest sickness.*

ISSUES THAT YOU CARRY INSIDE YOU WILL MAKE YOU DIS-AT-EASE—DISEASED.

What you don't confront will settle on the inside of you and will manifest sickness. The mind gets diseased and the body responds. Heal the mind and the body responds as well. Remember, every outcome depends on how we respond to events.

What are you speaking inside yourself? You can pray, but be praying the wrong way, and end up bringing a curse on yourself. In this way, your meditation is your medication. The patterns of thought and meditation you establish will determine your health and prosperity in body, mind and spirit. If you can put past pain to rest, focus on where you are now, and look with courage and faith toward the future, you will be healed.

The Key to Unlocking God's Intervention

That's the wonderful thing about systems. Security systems, financial systems, God's eternal system for manifestation—they all have keys. And once you master the use of that key, it always works. Millions of people have wondered what they had to do to attract the intervention of God in their affairs—to feel the work of God's hand helping their desires to manifest. In this last chapter of *The Laws of Thinking*, I am going to reveal to you this key, this secret of tapping the power that is God in every fiber of the world.

Are you prepared? Here it is—to activate the involvement of the Father, you must:

~

DREAM BIG ENOUGH TO NEED THE SUPERNATURAL INTERVENTION OF GOD.

~

That's it. Did you realize that God does not involve Himself in every single movement of every atom in this world? There are those who think that, but they mistake Spirit for God. Everything you see and touch is indeed Spirit, but it is not God. Spirit is the substance of God, but not God Himself. It is a kind of God-by proxy. There is no need for God to be involved when you are drinking a cup of coffee or reading a book. God does not interact with the events of your life until He needs to. That is what gives you the freedom to make choices.

But when you reach for the stars . . . when you dream on a grand scale and reach out with faith to create something audacious and unheard-of, you activate God's system. You set off a kind of cosmic alarm that demands God's supernatural intervention.

Dream big enough to need the supernatural events of God. When you put your faith on the line and give it a chance to work, God responds. When you do something that seems impossible, you require the supernatural hand of God to manifest results for you, because you have stated that you trust God enough to undertake this thing with no other option but God. Here's the fact, plain and simple:

~

GOD WANTS YOU TO THROW YOURSELF INTO A DILEMMA.

~

He wants you to sow yourself into an intervention—to take risks and sow your faith and give more than you can possibly afford. Then He steps in and brings down abundance on your head. That is when you will see miracles!

Failure Leads to a Bitter Harvest

You do not need to be wealthy. But the harvest for not fully manifesting and birthing the dream that God has planted in you is not simply lack of wealth. It is bitterness and anger for your entire life. That is the curse you afflict yourself with when you allow fear to stop you from throwing yourself into a dilemma and letting God pull you out.

If you don't take risks, you leave God out of the picture. Until there is uncertainty in your life, you will not see God. It is possible to budget God out of your life entirely, to play it so safe that God is never called to intervene in your affairs. When that happens, you will fail to birth the purpose that God had in mind for you. If you fail to birth, you will live in anger.

That is no way to live, let me tell you. When you have allowed fear to stunt the potential God placed in you, you will create your own Hell. You will lash out at others who are taking giant steps in your small world. You will start acting like a victim when you could have been a victor. That's why those who cannot be creators become critics: they need to break down those who have achieved what they could not so they can make themselves feel less impotent.

Your greatest enemies are those to whom you are a reminder of what they could have been. When you are successful, you will make enemies, because you will serve as a constant sting to the pride of those who could not achieve what you have achieved. No one wants a reminder of his failures.

Remember, there is no supernatural intervention from God in the safety zone. You have to sail away from shore. Double the dream you have been nurturing and your harvest will double!

Get in Your Right Mind

It seems that working in the system of God is full of pitfalls, and that's true. But there is a way to deal with them and avoid letting them sabotage all you are working to build:

∼

BECOME CLOTHED IN YOUR RIGHT MIND.

∼

Demons travel in partnerships; even devils know the importance of networking. They will assault you in the guise of people who are trying to help you, but who are really there to ruin what you have started to create. No one will be afraid of you when you are powerless, but they will be afraid of you when you become clothed in your Right Mind. Your Right Mind is the state of mind in which you are fully aware of the system of God and how to use it. When you are in your Right Mind, the system is *part of you!*

When you are the system, you become god. Then the demons of this world will fear you and stay away. But there is more to being in your Right Mind. You need

You can't handle millions of dollars with a $50,000- a-year mind.

a Right Mind to handle the prosperity that comes to you. You can't handle millions of dollars with a $50,000-a-year mind. You will have a mental breakdown! You must train your mind to contain the prosperity that God wants to heap upon you.

Lottery winners are perfect examples of people who are not in their Right Mind when prosperity comes to them by accident. In this case, prosperity can come from God or Satan, depending on your response. You have seen lottery winners who squandered their money, who broke up their families over it, and who ended up poor because their untrained minds did not know how to handle the wealth. They are like beginning martial artists who are suddenly granted the ability to kill with their bare hands. They will abuse the power. But a martial artist who spends years working to learn the disciplines of karate or aikido will also learn responsibility and restraint. He or she will learn the state of Right Mind and know how to use that wealth of physical knowledge—and how NOT to use it.

When you hit God's lottery, it comes after much work and testing, so you are ready. You are in your Right Mind, ready to recognize what comes and use it to the fullest effect to create blessings and glory. And you know to give the first fruits of your wealth to God.

The Poor Lack Management, Not Money

Here's something many folks won't like, but I'm not in the business of dispensing self-esteem. I'm in the business of revealing truth. So to the matter:

~

IN AMERICA, THERE ARE NO POOR PEOPLE.

~

America is a society that is designed for you to have capital. We all have the same potential to have capital. What the poor lack is not money, but *management*.

You can be here for 20 years and still not own a house, but an immigrant can come here for five years and own a house. The difference? Management! Your kid is floundering in school, while a kid who comes from Korea and doesn't speak English ends up as class valedictorian! The difference is management. You must have a system to manage the affairs of your life. You must stop making excuses and put away all things that do not serve your management system: people, drugs, debt, a poor job, the passivity of mind that is an offense to God.

How do you run the business of your life? The rich make decisions; they run their lives like businesses. The poor do not. The rich send their children to private boarding schools that make the students study for two hours every night before they can engage in any other activities. Those habits stay with those students for life, so that when they are in college and beyond, they know how to manage their time and their lives. Management means something very simple:

~

MANAGEMENT: THE APPLICATION OF YOUR TIME AND RESOURCES TO THOSE THINGS THAT

INCREASE YOUR PROSPERITY.

~

That's it. People who know how to manage their lives know what matters and what does not. They have a system that is automatic, so they can't waste time on things that are not from God. When you have a system, you cannot be late. You cannot fail. They never accept mediocrity, because they know that God does not accept it, either. God is only interested in your excellence.

Final Wisdom

God asks one more thing from you as you make this lifelong journey toward full realization of your divinity: pass it on. Teach your children the Laws of Thinking. Your children should outdo you. If they don't, you did something wrong. Your children should surpass you and you should take joy in it!

Teach your children to honor their parents. The only way to honor your parents is with money, as the only way you can honor God is with money. You can only honor God with your substance. A boy should begin learning to honor his mother with money when he is 12 or 13. He's old enough to work at that age. A boy who does not learn to honor his mother will not honor his wife.

Finally, respect that which is worth respecting. Find someone worthy of respect and pursuit. Treat them right. Treat money right. What you respect will come toward you. What you fail to respect, will become uncomfortable in your presence and it will leave. What you fail to take care of, you will lose. When you disrespect money, your ability to attract it will vanish. If you want to harvest, show respect.

Don't blame anything on a red man with a tail. Understand where the devil is and you can cast him out yourself. You are the key to creation. You are all you need to tap into the system of God and take your place as His divine co-Creator. You have eternal, unlimited potential waiting to be unlocked within your mind and Spirit. It is all up to you!

God believes in you as you believe in Him. Together, there is nothing you cannot dream or accomplish. Become the abundance you seek and manifest it.

Amen.

FREE WRITTEN PROPHECY

As seen on TV!

To get your free personal written word in the mail from me, Master Prophet E. Bernard Jordan simply visit our site at www.bishopjordan.com and follow the prompts. The Master Prophet will see the Mind of God on your behalf and he will give you the ANSWERS YOU HAVE BEEN SEEKING.

And be sure to listen to Bishop Jordan
on his weekly Hay House Radio program on
HayHouseRadio.com®

OTHER BOOKS BY
BISHOP E. BERNARD JORDAN

Achiever's Guide to Success
Breaking Soul Ties and Generational Curses
His Color Was Black: A Race Attack
Cosmic Economics
Cosmic Economics: The Universal Keys to Wealth Workbook
The Holy Spirit
"I AM" Mar Elijah the Root: Teaching on the Laws of the Spirit
The Joshua Generation
Keys to Liberation
The Making of the Dream
The Marital Union of Thought
The Mastery of Mentorship
Meditation: A Key to New Horizons in God
Mentoring: An Iconoclastic Approach to the Development of Ministry
Mentoring—The Missing Link
The Power of the Dime
The Power of Money
Praise & Worship
Prayer of Fasting
Prophetic Congress: Deep Calleth Upon Deep
Prophetic Congress: Deep Calleth Upon Deep *workbook*
Prophetic Congress "The Summit" Volume I)—Out of Print
Prophetic Congress "The Summit" Volume II)
Prophetic Genesis
The School of the Prophets Volume I
The School of the Prophets Volume II Hardcover
The School of the Prophets Volume II
The Science of Prophecy
The Science of Prophetic Leadership
The Seed of Destiny
Servanthood
The Spirit of Liberation
The Spirit of the Oppressor
Spiritual Protocol: A Supplement to, Mentoring—The Missing Link
Unveiling the Mysteries
What Every Woman Should Know About Men
Written Judgments Volume 1
Written Judgments Volume 2
Written Judgments Volume 3
Written Judgments Volume 4

Minibooks
Above All Things Get Wisdom
Calling Forth the Men of Valor
The Purpose of Tongues

We hope you enjoyed this Hay House book.
If you'd like to receive a free catalog featuring additional
Hay House books and products, or if you'd like information
about the Hay Foundation, please contact:

Hay House, Inc.
P.O. Box 5100
Carlsbad, CA 92018-5100

(760) 431-7695 or **(800) 654-5126**
(760) 431-6948 (fax) or **(800) 650-5115 (fax)**
www.hayhouse.com® • **www.hayfoundation.org**

Published and distributed in Australia by:
Hay House Australia Pty. Ltd., 18/36 Ralph St., Alexandria NSW 2015 •
Phone: 612-9669-4299 • *Fax:* 612-9669-4144 • www.hayhouse.com.au

Published and distributed in the United Kingdom by:
Hay House UK, Ltd., 292B Kensal Rd., London W10 5BE •
Phone: 44-20-8962-1230 • *Fax:* 44-20-8962-1239 • www.hayhouse.co.uk

Published and distributed in the Republic of South Africa by:
Hay House SA (Pty), Ltd., P.O. Box 990, Witkoppen 2068 •
Phone/Fax: 27-11-467-8904 • orders@psdprom.co.za • www.hayhouse.co.za

Published in India by:
Hay House Publishers India, Muskaan Complex, Plot No. 3, B-2,
Vasant Kunj, New Delhi 110 070 • *Phone:* 91-11-4176-1620 •
Fax: 91-11-4176-1630 • www.hayhouse.co.in

Distributed in Canada by:
Raincoast , 9050 Shaughnessy St., Vancouver, B.C. V6P 6E5 •
*Phone: (*604) 323-7100 • *Fax:* (604) 323-2600 • www.raincoast.com

Tune in to **HayHouseRadio.com®** for the best in inspirational talk radio
featuring top Hay House authors! And, sign up via the Hay House USA Website
to receive the Hay House online newsletter and stay informed about
what's going on with your favorite authors. You'll receive bimonthly
announcements about Discounts and Offers, Special Events,
Product Highlights, Free Excerpts, Giveaways, and more!
www.hayhouse.com®